T5-BPZ-869

INCONSISTENCIES

Studies in the New Testament, the
Inferno, Othello, and *Beowulf*

WILLIAM WHALLON

D. S. BREWER · BIBLIO

809
W552i

© William Whallon 1983

Published by D. S. Brewer
240 Hills Road Cambridge
an imprint of Boydell & Brewer Ltd
PO Box 9 Woodbridge Suffolk IP12 3DF
and by Biblio
81 Adams Drive, Totowa, New Jersey 07512, USA

First published 1983

British Library Cataloguing in Publication Data
Whallon, William
  Inconsistencies.
  1. Literature, Medieval   2 Inconsistency in
  literature   3. Bible. N. T.—Criticism,
  interpretation, etc.
  I. Title
  809'.92   PN682.I

  ISBN 0-85991-131-4

Library of Congress Cataloging in Publication Data
Whallon, William, 1928–
  Inconsistencies: studies in the New Testament,
the Inferno, Othello, and Beowulf.

  Bibliography: p.
  Includes indexes.
  1. Literature—History and criticism.   2. Hermeneutics.
3. Criticism, Textual.   4. Last Supper.   5. Dante
Alighieri, 1265–1321. Inferno.   6. Shakespeare,
William, 1564–1616. Othello.   7. Beowulf.   I. Title.
PN511.W49 1983   809   82-22807
ISBN 0-85991-131-4 (Biblio)

83-9059

Photoset by Rowland Phototypesetting Ltd
Bury St Edmunds, Suffolk
Printed in Great Britain by St Edmundsbury Press
Bury St Edmunds, Suffolk

Library of
Davidson College

INCONSISTENCIES

ALSO BY WILLIAM WHALLON

*Formula, Character, and Context: Studies in
Homeric, Old English, and Old Testament Poetry*

Problem and Spectacle: Studies in the Oresteia

Even today Melchizedek the priest
Commends to us tart vintage limpid red
Undrugged by sleepy myrrh, and wholesome bread
Incorrupt of the saprophytic yeast.
Is Christ a real presence within that feast?
Recall the baffling final things he said:
To empty death by raising up the dead
The son of man becomes a yearly beast.
I sign my heart this testament is true—
Not common truth such as pathfinders know,
Pawed by a sheriff bear, or sailors who
Hear the narwhal bellow his weal and woe;
But truth profound, as why the adepts hew
The star of David from a flake of snow.

W.W.

Preface

The literary anomaly is easy to find. In the Embassy to Achilles, in the *Iliad*, why does the poet, referring to three persons, repeatedly say "both of them"? When Hamlet speaks about "The undiscover'd country from whose bourn No traveller returns," has he forgotten the ghost of his father? Truly, there are inconsistencies galore. The ones dealt with here—the questions I try to answer with replies of my own—rank among the worthiest.

As a collection, the essays are intended to further comparative method. Part of my program has been to take chances; so the likelihood of basic error is high; "only those who do not work can be sure of not making mistakes" (Ginzburg, *Key Problems of Physics*, 2nd ed. p. 143). Seeing that what I have written I have written, some arguments from my two earlier volumes are used again, for different ends. The chapters have been read by Robert T. Anderson, John A. Yunck, Karl F. Thompson, and Robert J. Geist, respectively, and Michigan State University has been a silent partner, a friend indeed.

W.W.

East Lansing, Michigan   *June 1982*

Contents

I. The last supper and the meals of remembrance or fellowship

A. Was the fellowship meal known as a "(feast of) charity"?

There is disagreement on whether, when the New Testament was being put into writing, the ceremony now known as the ΑΓΑΠΗ— *agapē* "(feast of) charity," or fellowship meal—was distinct from, or continuous with, or another name for, the sacrament. Working backwards in time, we begin with Tertullian (*Apology* 39), who spoke of the agape explicitly, and did not connect it with the sacrament at all. Our next witness, one more valuable because less friendly, is Pliny, who similarly kept the agape wholly separate from any sacrament: Christians swore that

> the height of their fault or error was as follows. They would meet on a fixed day before dawn and chant by turns a song to Christ as if to a god. Then they would pledge themselves solemnly not to commit thievery or robbery or adultery, nor to be false to a trust, nor to deny a deposit when it was asked for again. Afterwards they would break up, and later come together for a meal, a common and harmless one. (*Letters* 10.96, to Trajan)

If there is a sacrament here, it is the rite at daybreak; the food with comradeship is the agape; or else we have been misled.

Meanwhile, the martyr Ignatius (his letter to the *Romans* 7.3) was writing that for food he desired the bread of God which is the flesh of Christ, and for wine, his blood which is incorruptible love. The last word here is *agapē*: do we catch an allusion to the feast of charity? or to the sacrament? or are these the very same? or is there no allusion at all? Earlier still, the apostle Paul was perhaps

9

referring to the agape as an adjunct to the sacrament, in his censure of those whose manners were unseemly:

> When ye come together therefore into one place, this is not to eat the Lord's supper. For in eating every one taketh before other his own supper: and one is hungry, and another is drunken. What? have ye not houses to eat and to drink in? or despise ye the church of God, and shame them that have not? What shall I say to you? shall I praise you in this? I praise you not. (1 Cor. 11.20–22)

The passage, though by no means a fine composition, is of special interest, seeing that what follows is a brief account of the last supper and its commemoration. *The Oxford Dictionary of the Christian Church* calls these verses the classical reference to the agape in the New Testament; but the term itself is not used.

The only biblical instances of *agapē* in the sense "feast of charity"—rather than simply "charity" or "love"—are Jude 12 and perhaps 2 Peter 2.13. Codex Sinaiticus has ΑΓΑΠΗ at Jude 12, and ΑΠΑΤΗ "deception" at 2 Peter 2.13. Codex Vaticanus has ΑΓΑΠΗ for both; Codex Alexandrinus, ΑΠΑΤΗ for both. The Authorized Version, the Revised Standard Version, the Jerusalem Bible, the Anchor Bible, and the New English Bible, all follow the Codex Sinaiticus. But one of the words must be responsible for the other. They resemble each other too closely, and their passages—Jude 4–13 and 2 Peter 2.1–17—are too similar, to be independent. The change may have been an error or it may have been made on purpose. Which text is the better?

> These are spots in your feasts of charity (Jude 12, A.V.)

> Spots they are and blemishes, sporting themselves with their own deceivings (2 Pet. 2.13, A.V.)

> These are blemishes on your love feasts (Jude 12, R.S.V.)

> They are blots and blemishes, reveling in their dissipation (2 Pet. 2.13, R.S.V.)

They are a dangerous obstacle to your community meals (Jude 12, Jer.B.)

They are unsightly blots on your society . . . and they amuse themselves deceiving you (2 Pet. 2.13, Jer.B.)

These are the hidden reefs at your love meals (Jude 12, Anch.B.)

they are blots and blemishes, reveling in their dissipations (2 Pet. 2.13, Anch.B.)

These men are a blot on your love-feasts (Jude 12, N.E.B.)

they are an ugly blot on your company, because they revel in their deceptions (2 Pet. 2.13, N.E.B.)

ΟΥΤΟΙ ΕΙΣΙΝ ΕΝ ΤΑΙΣ ΑΓΑΠΑΙΣ ΥΜΩΝ ΣΠΙΛΑΔΕΣ (Jude 12, ed. Tasker)

ΣΠΙΛΟΙ ΚΑΙ ΜΩΜΟΙ ΕΝΤΡΥΦΩΝΤΕΣ ΕΝ ΤΑΙΣ ΑΠΑΤΑΙΣ ΑΥΤΩΝ (2 Pet. 2.13, ed. Tasker)

It looks as if *apatē* "deception" could more easily be replaced by *agapē* "feast of charity" in 2 Peter than the contrary could be done in Jude. So which word, or which text, would seem the source of the other? Without going further we should say that *agapē* and Jude 12 were the originals.

The matter is complicated by the disputed word *spilas* near by in Jude 12. It means "blemish" or the like according to some versions, but "reef" or the like according to others. Can the issue be decided from 2 Peter 2.13? There the *spilas*—appearing as *spilos*, a masculine for a feminine—has a synonym added, so that the sense is "blemish and blot" or the like. Such doublets are common in the Old Testament, and this very one may be found in Numbers 19.2 (the Hebrew text; not the Septuagint, which uses a single term twice; cf. 1 Pet. 1.19, 2 Pet. 3.14). So the phrase of 2 Peter 2.13 looks ordinary, and may therefore have been the original, not the copy. The word in Jude 12 would then without doubt have the sense "blemish."

Expansion is more usual than contraction, though, especially when the thought is obscure, for those who express strange ideas are apt to amplify them. For this reason, as well as from a consideration of *agapē*, we should believe that the likelier original was Jude 12. So what is our choice, for that verse, between "reef" and "blemish"? Since copyists tend to change a rare word or meaning into a common one, and since the usual sense of *spilas* in other authors is "reef," not "blemish," the direction of error would have been towards "reef," not towards "blemish." So if the copy has the harder alternative—if 2 Peter 2.13 has "blemish"—it is probably sound. The results are pleasing: we have an interesting sense rather than a routine one; we have the interesting sense accommodated, "blemish" going with "blot" as smoothly as "wine" with "strong drink"; and we have an argument that the writer of 2 Peter 2.13, as an interpreter of Jude 12, knew the Greek of his day at least as well as we do.

The phrase remains a tough one to chew and digest. "Sacrifice without spot" is of course powerful; "commandment without spot" (1 Tim. 6.14) may be comprehensible; but "spots on a feast"—referring not to the blemishes on an imperfect lamb or kid, but to persons who are a criminal nuisance—is a challenge. Nor are parallel instances of the word very helpful. Liddell and Scott, as early as 1880 if not before, cited a line from the *Lithica* of "Orpheus" where *spilas*, in a description of the agate, denotes a spot or marking on a stone. Bigg—in the International Critical Commentary edition of Jude, in 1901—took up the reference, and gave the sense as "dappled with spots." Still, the expression "spots (flaws, blemishes, blots) on a *feast*" is not one that anybody would ever use.

I have been at pains to divulge my solution in the words immediately preceding. For ΑΓΑΠΗ in Jude read ΑΧΑΤΗ "agate." The passage then says that the hooligans at the fellowship meal are "moles in a gemstone," a proverbial comparison like "flies in the ointment." Either a scribe seeing the "agate" in a document, or an amanuensis hearing it dictated, wrought the mistake, almost surely because he did not see or hear the word correctly, though

12

possibly because he did not understand it. With whatever motive, the word was written as *agapē*, which until then had meant only "love" or "charity," not a meal of any kind. The author of 2 Peter, making use of Jude (or proto-Jude), changed the *agapē* into *apatē*, which he would not have done if *agapē* had been intelligible, as it would have been if it had already alluded in some way to eating. This reconstruction of mine depends on deduction, some might say guesswork, and I am willing to yield on the details. The reading AXATH does however strike me as certain.

There was no "feast of charity," no fellowship meal called an *agapē*, until Jude 12—possibly with the concurrence of 2 Peter 2.13 but probably not—could be read as we have it. Gatherings with bread and wine and fishes, modelled on the gospel incidents, had been regular all along, but they had not been known as "loves" or "charities." When the new name took hold, it no doubt affected practice. In his use of *agapē* Tertullian was furthering an error, one that did more good than harm until the custom was given up, but an error nevertheless. The list of names for meals and rites in biblical times—*agapē*, Lord's supper, breaking of bread, eucharist—must be diminished by one.

B. Was the last supper, was Jesus on the cross, a passover?

1. The passover lamb, the passover bread

The people of a book—such as Jews, Christians, and Moslems—have to decide just how sacred their book may be. If you say "that God is the author of Holy Scripture" (from the encyclical *Humani Generis* of Pius XII, delivered 12 August 1950), then do you say that scripture is flawless because God is flawless? To alter a letter or two—as with ΑΓΑΠΗ, ΑΠΑΤΗ, AXATH—will perhaps be allowed; but what about whole verses, whole episodes? Barr (*Fundamentalism* pp. 56–57 for the examples following) has shown at what cost the bible can be thought inerrant. Did Jesus cleanse the temple towards the very end of his ministry as the synoptic gospels have it (Mt 21.12–17, Mk 11.15–19, Lk 18.45–46), or towards the very beginning as the fourth gospel has it (Jn 2.13–25)? Can the fact be that he cleansed the temple twice? Did then Jesus ascend to heaven twice, once on the day of resurrection (Lk 24.50–53), once forty days later (Acts 1.9–12)? The moral is, acknowledge that there are discrepancies, and forbear to heal them with a remedy worse than the ailment.

Was the last supper a passover meal, or was Jesus on the cross a passover sacrifice (killed at the customary hour)? The synoptic gospels and the Western church favour the one answer; the fourth gospel and the Eastern church, the other. There is agreement that all the events from the last supper through the crucifixion took place on a single day (by the reckoning then in use)—after the sunset closing Thursday and before the sunset closing Friday. Whether the passover was on this day, or on the following one (a sabbath), is the matter at issue.

The passover means first of all the lamb. According to tradition, the Israelites in Egypt were bidden to kill a lamb, and to smear every house of theirs with its blood, so that the Lord might "pass over the door" of any family that belonged to him (Ex. 12.21–23). The commemoration is a *thank* offering for the deliverance. Segal *Hebrew Passover* finds, though, that some verses speak about keeping the passover with a massive holocaust of bullocks and rams as a *sin* offering (Eze. 45.22–23); "as at the Arab *fedu* sacrifices, the blood was smeared on the house to make atonement for all its inmates" (Segal p. 105, cf. 6, 164). Who were smitten among the Egyptians, but not among the Israelites? The firstborn. So in time to come the firstborn more than others might think themselves bought at the cost of the annual lamb. But "whatsoever openeth the womb" (Ex. 13.2)—especially every male: every firstborn son (Ex. 22.29) and every firstling male of herd or flock (Ex. 34.19, Deut. 15.19)—had already in an earlier era (to judge from the story of Isaac) been sanctified unto the Lord, and was to be sacrificed or else redeemed with a lamb. The feast is then a *homage* offering, by affinity and association. To separate the strands—of thanks, sin, and homage—is a scholarly activity, not a liturgical one. But so close on all accounts is the lamb to the heart of the ritual, it may itself be called the passover (Ex. 12.21).

Secondly, the passover means the unleavened bread. The Israelites "baked unleavened cakes of the dough which they brought forth out of Egypt, for it was not leavened; because they were thrust out of Egypt, and could not tarry" (Ex. 12.34–39). The commemoration will again be a *thank* offering. But—being most holy, uncontaminated—the unleavened bread is also associated with a *sin* offering (Lev. 6.16, Segal 168). And, because during the holiday a sheaf of firstfruits was laid on the altar, the unleavened bread has to do with a *homage* offering besides (Lev. 23.10, Segal 30). A braid of motives, as before. The lamb is eaten once only; the unleavened bread is eaten for a week. The greater element is the lamb; the lamb is the passover, and the feast in its entirety is the passover; but an alternative name for the passover is the feast of the unleavened bread (Ex. 12.17).

In the fourth gospel Jesus is "the Lamb of God, which taketh away the sin of the world" (1.29). A firstborn male, "only begotten son" (3.16), he is crucified on the afternoon before the passover feast, just when the passover lambs are killed (13.1, 19.31). Not a bone of him is broken (19.33) as not a bone of the passover lamb is to be broken (Ex. 12.46, Num. 9.12).

In the synoptic gospels the passover is the feast of the un-leavened bread, *ta azuma* (Mt 26.17, Mk 14.12, Lk 22.7). The word used presently, though—as if the flight from Egypt were no longer remembered—is *artos*, ordinary bread (Mt 26.26, Mk 14.22, Lk 22.19). The lamb is not spoken of: *Hamlet* without the prince (Nineham ed. *Mark* p. 457 n.). In the absence of the lamb we gather that the phrasing—"they killed the passover" (Mk 14.12), "the passover must be killed" (Lk 22.7, cf. Mt 26.19)—has lost its original sense and been kept for the sake of ritual. The meaning is not that a beast shall be slaughtered, but that the fare—called the passover—shall be special food. The bread is then in some way Jesus, at the feast of the unleavened bread, which is called the passover. It is a sin offering, at least by one interpretation (Mt 26.28, cf. Mk 14.24, Lk 22.20), not a thank offering or a homage offering. Now in one way, now in another—the lamb in the fourth gospel, the bread in the synoptic gospels—the passover is alluded to; but a new significance has replaced the old.

In 1 Corinthians 11.23–25 the last supper—" . . . my body . . . my blood"—is that of the synoptic gospels. The passover (in any sense) is not mentioned, but can be taken from 1 Corinthians 5.6–8:

> Know ye not that a little leaven leaveneth the whole lump? Purge out therefore the old leaven that ye may be a new lump, as ye are unleavened. For even Christ our passover is sacrificed for us; therefore let us keep the feast, not with old leaven, neither with the leaven of malice and wickedness; but with the unleavened bread of sincerity and truth.

Richardson *Mass and Lord's Supper* p. 689 believes that the central verse of this passage means, "Christ has been sacrificed as our paschal lamb." To me it all makes better sense if the passover means (unleavened) bread; so I would again take "passover is sacrificed" for no more than a hallowed phrase. The apostle is then arguably in accord with the synoptic evangelists. To say that he influenced them would seem unwarranted though, seeing that the epistles and the gospels have little else in common.

Matthew, Mark, Luke, and evidently Paul have the one image of Jesus as passover; John has the other, and so possibly does the book of Acts: "And we sailed away from Philippi after the days of unleavened bread, and came unto them to Troas in five days; where we abode seven days" (20.6). How could any Christian mention the feast of the unleavened bread without alluding to Jesus? It might be done if Jesus were thought of as the passover lamb, and if the lamb were somehow not thought to be a sacrifice at the feast of the unleavened bread. I do not see in the biblical materials, then, any way of arguing back to the last supper, to determine which day it took place on.

Jeremias *Eucharistic Words*—besides offering several theorems of his own, together with objections against them—reviews the two possibilities, and in an appendix musters the scholars who have spoken for the one or for the other. Is there a third, a fourth possibility? Yes, perhaps both traditions are true, perhaps neither is. For Jude 12 and 2 Peter 2.13 we were choosing among ΑΓΑΠΗ (as in the Codex Vaticanus), ΑΠΑΤΗ (as in the Codex Alexandrinus), both (as in the Codex Sinaiticus), and neither (but ΑΧΑΤΗ instead). Our problem now—the day of the Passover—is similar, though weightier: (1) is the fourth gospel right, or (2) are the synoptic gospels right, or (3) are they somehow both right, or (4) is neither right?

Jeremias sums up in his text the case for both days, and names in his appendix the scholar or two who argue for neither day. How *both* days? how can the gospel accounts be harmonized? An older thesis, which Jeremias is sorry to find fault with, has the Pharisees observing the passover on the one day, the Sadducees on the other. A newer thesis by Jaubert—in *Revue de l'histoire des religions* 146:140–173—would distinguish between the solar and the official calendars, but has not been corroborated as it ought to have. Why then *neither* day? why would anybody refuse to accept either? The aperçu of Bertram—*Leidengeschichte Jesu* p. 32 n. 1—is that the evangelists, looking backwards upon the life of Jesus from their worship of him, dated by passover typology.

Surely these last few words, loosening the problem by literary criticism rather than by historical research, have the answer, do they not? I myself believe so, and would supplement them with an argument about the influence of the Old Testament in Greek.

2. The etymologizing of *pascha* and the gospels

The Old Testament is notorious for its explanations of names. Abram "a lofty father," from 'āb + rûm, becomes (Gen. 17.5) Abraham "father of many nations," from 'āb + hāmōn + an -r- unaccounted for. Similarly with the ancient and modern etymologies of the root psḥ. None is wholly satisfactory (Segal *Hebrew Passover* pp. 95–106); and the most fanciful of all is the one given in Exodus 12.11–13: the Lord would *pass over* (pāsaḥ) those whose houses had been smeared; for is not such smearing customary at the *passover* (pesaḥ)? Note how fortunate our translation is! what good luck it was that we could, almost, keep the name psḥ in

English, and translate it besides! What other language allows the same? Greek nearly does, though not quite. By changing the sense from "I will pass over you" (Ex. 12.13) to "I will *shelter* you," the Septuagint is able to work the *pas-* into its verb *skepasō*, while it transliterates (the Aramaic form of) the noun as *pascha*. (The *-k-* or *sk-* of *skepasō* even answers to the *-ch-* or *-sch-* of *pascha*, at least remotely.) An ingenious and admirable rendering, which makes the Semitic word more intelligible. Still, in all other contexts *pascha* would, to a Greek mind, have sounded foreign. How was it to be understood in everyday life? It was to be etymologized anew.

"The word derives from what happened," says Melito (paragr. 46, cf. Irenaeus in Migne *PG* 7.1000, Justin Martyr *PG* 6.561): *apo tou pathein to paschein* "from *pathein* ('to endure the passion') comes *paschein* ('to sacrifice the passover')." The noun *pascha*, Aramaic transliterated into Greek, is here made into a verb, "to sacrifice the passover"; but the verb already existed, the present tense of the aorist *pathein* "to suffer"; *paschein* is a fusion of the two. Is the author sincere in this word-play? Yes, it is a sermon not just upon words, but upon ideas.

Augustine takes the type to be the Israelites' passing over the Red Sea on the way to the promised land, and the antitype to be Jesus' passing over from this life into the next (*PL* 35.1785, cf. 36.842, 37.1832, 38.616, all commenting on John 13.1, "Now before the feast of the passover, when Jesus knew that his hour was come that he should depart out of this world unto the Father"; see Mohrmann in *Ephemerides Liturgicae* 66:37–52). Hardly; Augustine is aligning two events, one from the Old Testament, the other from the New; but the fact is, the passover commemorates that smeared doors were passed over, not that the Red Sea was. No, the real challenge is from the Greek theologians Gregory of Nazianzus and Procopius of Gaza (in Migne *PG* 36,636, 87.561; see the Lampe lexicon), who regard *pascha* . . . *paschein* as mere Hellenizing, not as a truth. Can we in their despite find the etymology, rather than the typology alone, in the gospels?

Yes, so long as we hold—with Black *Aramaic Approach* 2nd ed. pp. 206–211—that the evangelists used Greek materials as well as Aramaic ones, and that the gospels were to be Hellenistic rather than Palestinian books (for persons who thought in Greek rather than in Aramaic, and who would read the Septuagint rather than the Hebrew scriptures). Luke 22.15 has Jesus say, "With desire I have desired *to eat of this passover* with you *before I suffer"* . . . *to pascha phagein . . . pro tou me pathein*, where the etymology is nearly as audible as in Melito's *apo tou pathein to paschein* (so Eutychius in Migne *PG* 86.2393 on the verse). (Mt 26.2, replacing *suffer* with *be crucified*, has a more powerful verb, but still weakens the phrase; it is as if one were to tamper with *la'ilaha ill'Allah*.) Dalman, who translated the words of Jesus back into Aramaic, discovering their paronomasia and rhetorical force, thought (*Jesus—Jeshua* pp. 127–128) that *to pascha phagein . . . pro tou me pathein* "to eat this passover . . . before I suffer" (Lk 22.15) would be an unusual expression in Aramaic, because *suffer* has no object. Accordingly, this one saying was not Aramaic in origin; its paronomasia—*pascha* within *pathein (paschein)*—was Greek to begin with. (The noun *epithumia* "desire" at the start of the verse may then be traced back to, and thought an equivalent of, the *spoudē* of Ex. 12.11, which translates the un-ambiguous Hebrew ḥipāzôn "haste," but may itself mean either "haste" or "zeal, desire.") Do we have here, in the etymology, a belief common to all four gospels? That is the sum of what I would urge. The fortuitous likeness between Semitic psḥ and Greek *paschein* was the forebear of the idea, not merely a midwife to the idea, that Jesus was the passover. In one way he was the lamb that taketh away sin; in another, his body was the bread.

Richardson *Mass and Lord's Supper*, who represents thoughtful present-day opinion, sees (1) that the etymology was accepted by Melito and other Greek-speaking apologists of the early centuries (p. 485), and (2) that the typology, known to Paul, profoundly influenced both the synoptic and the fourth gospels, in different ways (pp. 689–693). So how does my discussion vary from his? On (1): Richardson tells of the etymologizing that was done after, I tell of that which was done before, the gospels were written. Whereas "psḥ from psḥ" makes sense, as *passover* from *pass over* does, the rendering in the Septuagint—*pascha* from *skepasō*—does not make sense so easily; *pascha* was strange as a Greek word if it were not otherwise explained. On (2): Richardson takes *pascha* in Greek to mean the passover lamb only, so that for the synoptic gospels the idea "Christ our passover is sacrificed" (1 Cor. 5.7) can hardly combine with the idea "the bread . . . is it not . . . the body of Christ?" (1 Cor. 10.16). I take *pascha* in Greek to mean the lamb and the bread equally well; "sacrifice the passover" in the synoptic gospels is no more than a timeworn expression for "prepare the passover meal."

A second bridge between the testaments is the divine name. Because the commandment forbade taking the name in vain, the consonants Yhwh in the Old Testament were written with the vowels of *Adonai* "Lord," and the name would be pronounced "Adonai." The Septuagint rendered it accordingly as *kurios*, the common noun meaning "lord" in Greek. As a title *kurios* was used also, in New Testament times, for persons of rank, such as Pilate. And in special ways it was used by his disciples for Jesus (see Beare *Matthew* p. 42). Were not then God and Jesus to fuse, at least in the minds of some? To a Christian hearing *kurios* read from the Septuagint, Father and Son became, if not identical, at least hard to distinguish between. What was the sense when *kurios* was combined with *pascha*? Would it not be doubly twofold?

> And thus shall ye eat it; with your loins girded, your shoes on your feet, and your staff in your hand; and ye shall eat it in haste: it is the Lord's passover (*pascha esti kuriōi*, Ex. 12.11)

> In one night shall ye eat it by household and by tribe, with your loins girded, and your staff in your hand. For this is the Lord's passover (*pascha kuriou*), an enduring memorial to the children of Israel (Melito 13)

> Salvation is made manifest, and the apostles are given understanding. The Lord's passover proceeds (*kuriou pascha*). Candles are brought forward and there is harmony in arrangement. And, teaching the saints, the Word is gladdened, through whom the Father is glorified, to whom be glory through the ages (to Diognetus in Migne *PG* 2.1185)

The dative *kuriōi* in the Exodus verse means *unto* the Lord; the genitive *kuriou* in Melito means *belonging to*, but shades into *consisting in*, the sense it has in the letter to Diognetus, where the reference is no longer to the passover at all, but to the Easter celebration. The words *(kurios, pascha)* singly, and the phrase *(pascha kuriou)* in its entirety, had come to say one thing for the old covenant and another for the new (these being sometimes heard together). And what *pascha* said for the new—Jesus the passover lamb, the passover bread—was *paschein*.

To sum up: (1) *pascha* "passover" in the Septuagint was a foreign word, therefore meaningless, susceptible to being understood from *paschein* "suffer"; (2) Melito (and Irenaeus and Justin) in fact explained the word so; (3) Luke by implication did so too, giving us the warrant for saying that—the thesis of my essay—Jesus became the passover by *etymological* typology; (4) to see how the new sense of *pascha* might combine with the old, consider the phrase "the Lord's passover" in Exodus and in patristic writing.

We began with the question: What was the date of the passover? Neither alternative—John on the one hand; Matthew, Mark, and Luke on the other—would now be adequate. We would rather say: It is a matter of story, not of history; and both accounts have truth in them. To confirm this argument, even indirectly, will be difficult, though. I believe our best course is a study of how an idea elsewhere could be simultaneously developed in different ways.

3. Comparable instances of word illustration

That Jesus is the passover (the lamb or the unleavened bread) at passover season, how shall we account for it? By comparison with a series of ironies in Homeric poetry. The chief figures in the *Iliad* and the *Odyssey* are characterized, to a degree, in accord with the epithets attached to their names. Diomedes more than anyone else is called a tamer of horses, and among the horsemen at Troy he is the ablest. He captures a pair of the legendary horses of Tros (*Il.* 5.265–327), and wins glory with them in both warfare (8.106–121) and athletics (23.291–513). Apollo has a number of titles meaning bowman. So it is fitting, when he would avenge his priest, that he should come from Olympus with bow and arrows, striking first the mules and the dogs but then the men (1.37–50), and it is fitting that those who want success in archery should pray to him (4.119–121, 23.861–881). These are among the cardinal ironies of literature; the epithets have been worked out in episodes. If we were able to tell how it happened—if we could say why Odysseus with bow and arrows slays the suitors on the feast day of Apollo (*Od.* 20.276–278, 21.258, 22.1–7)—we might be able to comment on the irony of the passover.

When an epithet—describing Diomedes as a tamer of horses, or Apollo as an archer—answers not to just a single episode but to a number of them, we ask, Did the epithet generate the episodes, or was it generated by them? It is easier to believe that the epithet became pictured in several episodes than to believe that several episodes together gave single voice to the epithet. That the style influenced the content is likelier than the contrary. Diomedes is a horseman in episodes because he was a tamer of horses by epithet. Similarly for Jesus as the passover. At first it was a matter of language, not an image. Afterwards—as if for illustration—he became now the lamb, now the unleavened bread.

Jesus was now the passover lamb, now the passover bread. The two conceptions must have been worked out together, for each tradition has a trace of the other. In the fourth gospel—though not in the synoptics, where he is nevertheless the passover bread—he is the bread of life (Jn 6.35–48–58). In the synoptics—though not in the fourth gospel, where he is nevertheless the passover lamb—he gives up the ghost at the ninth hour (Mt 27.46, Mk 15.34, Lk 23.44–46), when the passover lambs were killed (Philo, Loeb ed. Suppl. vol. 2 p. 20; Segal *Hebrew Passover* p. 34 n. 12, p. 246; Driver ed. *Exodus* on Ex. 12.6). The ideas have evidently not been fully developed. The reference to the ninth hour—though very fine in Matthew, Mark, and Luke—would have been finer yet in John. The verses about the bread of life—though meaningful in John—might have been yet more so in Matthew, Mark, and Luke.

The New Testament illustrates the image "Jesus the passover" in different ways. And so at times does Homeric poetry with the images in its epithets. Ajax is *telamōnios*, an adjective from the noun *telamōn*, and the description is a good one in three ways. He is a telamon in the sense of column, gigantic and immobile; he wears an old-fashioned body shield with a conspicuous telamon or strap crossing over the left shoulder; and he is the son of a man named Telamon. Why choose among these meanings? why not accept them all? Similarly for "Jesus the passover lamb" in the fourth gospel and "Jesus the passover bread" in the synoptic gospels. Both meanings of "Jesus the passover" are fine; their being at odds is no matter.

Why is it called the passover? "Because the Lord passed over the houses that had been smeared, and because the Israelites passed over the Red Sea." Actually, only the first is from Exodus, the second is from Augustine; so the bible cannot be faulted. Why was not the bread leavened? "The people took their dough before it was leavened, their kneadingtroughs being bound up in their clothes upon their shoulders" (Ex. 12.34), "and they baked unleavened cakes of the dough which they brought forth out of Egypt, for it was not leavened; because they were thrust out of Egypt, and could not tarry" (verse 39). This truly is a near instance of superjustification. The dough was not leavened since the troughs were packed *and* since there would be no time for dough to rise. The accounts may be harmonized: the troughs were packed *because* there would be no time for dough to rise. But scripture itself gives the two reasons without reconciling them. Why is Hector described in Homeric poetry as the man "with the glancing helmet"? Does the epithet refer to a nodding horsehair plume, or to flashing plates of metal? Surely it does not refer to both at once? Well, Hector's baby son was frightened by the plume as it nodded terribly from the crest, and then Hector took off the helmet and laid it, shining brightly, on the ground (*Il.* 6.470–473). Again, while either explanation would have sufficed, the two are more than sufficient. Likewise for the gospels with their passover. In John, if more were said of Jesus as the bread of life, there would be a conflict with his being not the passover bread, but the lamb. In Matthew, Mark, and Luke, if more were said about why the

23

heavens should have been dark at the ninth hour, we might reflect that a passover meal without the lamb had been shared the night before.

Some items about Jesus are primary; some are secondary, early or late; some are tertiary. *Primary*, What he was heard to say, and seen to do, and thought to be, by those who knew him. *Secondary*, What was truly or falsely recounted about him—minus all that was forgotten about him or suppressed—by those who retold the story of his life or wrote it down: *early* secondary, fundamentals; *late* secondary, elaborations. *Tertiary*, What was subsequently realized to have been his significance and nature. Two groups of scholars—following either the fourth gospel or the synoptic gospels—hold that the death of Jesus *at the time of the passover* is primary: the feast was to occur a few hours after the crucifixion, or else it occurred with the last supper; Jesus might be thought of (by the one calculation) as the passover lamb, or else (by the other) as the unleavened passover bread. Really, neither allusion to the passover is primary, both are secondary, *late* secondary. What might be primary or early secondary would be a common source.

Scholars agree in taking the etymology *pascha . . . paschein* to be tertiary, as belonging to the corpus of comments and homilies by the church fathers. I take it to be *early* secondary, as the reason why Jesus is the passover. One tradition, that behind John, developed it in one way; another tradition—behind Matthew, Mark, and Luke—in another. (Just as "horse-taming" for Diomedes, and "far-shooting" for Apollo, have become scenes of moment.) The gist of my argument is that *pascha . . . paschein*—which made sense of the most obscure common noun in the Greek Old Testament, and made special sense of the phrase "the pascha of the Lord"—became illustrated in two of the greatest among all images, Jesus as lamb and as unleavened bread.

C. Was the last supper meant to be renewed in remembrance?

1. The first other era: the life to come

The fourth gospel ends by saying that "there are also many other things which Jesus did, the which, if they should be written every one, I suppose that even the world itself cound not contain the books that should be written." What were these other things that Jesus did? Was one of them to institute—with the words "in remembrance"—the ritual of the Lord's supper? The fourth gospel does not have those words. Nor do the synoptic gospels have them (except in a verse that some of the best authorities would reject). The undisputed, or less disputed, occurrence of the words is in 1 Corinthians 11. How could such a thing be omitted? but why would it have been added? We wish to know whether, and in what manner, the "in remembrance" is genuine.

The argument here will be that the accounts of the last supper are affined to matters of three other eras. The first of these, the subject following immediately, is the life to come. The second is the era of the old covenant. The third—which has not been paid its due—is the time of waiting.

The meal of the Essenes—the people of the Dead Sea scrolls, perhaps hasidim—may be regarded as "a liturgical anticipation of the Messianic banquet" promised in Isaiah 25.6–8: so Cross *Ancient Library of Qumran* p. 65, cf. 178, from whom I take what follows:

> This is the order of the feast for the communal council: the priest shall bless the first portion of the bread and the wine; next all the congregation shall give thanks and partake, each according to his rank, when as many as ten solemnly meet together. (condensed)

Did not Jesus and his disciples, in all their common meals, follow such customs? There would have been a master, a blessing, and the elements bread and wine (at the last supper in the fourth gospel the morsel—*psōmion*, the modern Greek word for bread—must have

25

been dipped in wine, to judge from Ruth 2.14). There would also have been the ten or more, and there might even have been the awareness of rank, a contention about lieutenancy or sergeancy, "a strife among them, which of them should be accounted the greatest" (Lk 22.24, cf. 14.8–10 not as in the Authorized Version).

Likewise with the words "our daily bread," which mean "our bread of the morrow," or "of the Morrow," the bread of life (Jeremias *Prayers of Jesus* p. 100). And likewise with the *eucharist*, or giving of thanks, in the *Didache*: the wine and bread are blessed in Jesus' name before the meal (paragr. 9), and then again afterwards (paragr. 10), with a comparison to spiritual fare, and with a wish that this world may pass away. Jesus' vow of abstinence—that he will not again drink wine until it is with the disciples in heaven (Mt 26.29, Mk 14.25, Lk 22.16–18)—looks then to the banquet beyond, and is not unique in doing so.

2. The second other era: the old covenant

"All thing must be fulfilled, which were written in the law of Moses, and in the prophets, and in the psalms" (Lk 24.44). Here lies the second and chief affinity of the last supper with matters of another era. The writings in prose (the five books of Moses and much else, including a great deal from the prophets)—being specific about persons and events, and being expressed in low style—were now seen to narrate forehappenings. The writings in poetry (the finest part of the prophets, almost the entirety of the psalms, and much else)—being philosophical rather than historical, being expressed in high style, and consisting solely of speech—were now thought to publish foretellings.

The procedure of the evangelists is partly a bookish, scholarly one, partly a nonscholarly remembering of an isolated detail or phrase. Sometimes they cite a source; sometimes not, leaving us to search. Of the collections that were to be fulfilled—the law of Moses, the prophets, and the psalms—the first is represented in the Exodus 12 account of the passover, which we have already considered. What remains is to study a passage from the prophets, namely Isaiah 53, and then one from the psalms, namely 41.9.

It must be laid down beforehand that the fulfilment may be highly creative. Consider the thirty pieces of silver, the treasury, the potter, and his field, in Matthew 27.3–10 (my comments deriving wholly from Strauss *A New Life of Jesus* 1865 trans., vol. 2 pp. 350–352):

> Then Judas . . . repented himself, and brought again the thirty pieces of silver to the chief priests and elders . . . And they said, What is that to us? . . . And he cast down the pieces of silver in the temple . . . and went and hanged himself. And the chief priests took the silver pieces, and said, It is not lawful for to put them into the treasury, because it is the price of blood. And they . . . bought with them the potter's field, to bury strangers in . . . Then was fulfilled that which was spoken by Jeremy the prophet, saying, And they took the thirty pieces of silver, the price of him that was valued . . . And gave them for the potter's field. . . .

The gospel refers to Jeremiah, who has indeed a parable of a potter (18.2–6). The passage adapted though is from Zechariah 11.13, and it concerns the price of a man: "And I took the thirty pieces of silver, and cast them to the potter in the house of the Lord." Here the word yāṣar "potter" does not make sense, for there is no potter in the house of the Lord that one would cast silver to. Surely it is a scribal mistake for 'ôṣār "treasury." Which variant did the evangelist use? He used them both! he found a role for the potter and one for the treasury as well! It is as if the elements had been assembled in a dream. Finally, the verse "this man purchased a field with the reward of iniquity, and falling headlong, he burst asunder" (the death of Judas as told in Acts 1.18) is the source of the potter's *field*!

It must also be laid down, as another preliminary principle, that several phrases or ideas from a single passage may be fulfilled, one of them being primary, the others secondary. Accordingly, when Jesus was crucified, Psalms 22.16 "they pierced my hands and my feet" came to mind, and the story of his death then became "a Christian dramatization" of the psalm in its entirety (Bundy *Jesus and the First Three Gospels* p. 536). The individual verses—

22.1 My God, my God, why hast thou forsaken me?

22.7 All they that see me laugh me to scorn

22.8 He trusted on the Lord that he would deliver him: let him deliver him, seeing he delighted in him

22.14 I am poured out like water

22.18 They part my garments among them, and cast lots upon my vesture

—all come true at least once in Matthew 27, Mark 15, Luke 23, and John 19. A corollary is that yet other verses from the psalm—such as "Many bulls have compassed me: strong bulls of Bashan have beset me round"—do not come true at all.

With these two principles—that the fulfilling of what was written may be creative; and that several elements from a passage may be fulfilled, one of them being primary, causing the others to follow—we shall the more acutely see that the gospels have completed not only certain forehappenings in the law, but also certain foretellings in the prophets and the psalms. Were all the fulfilments compatible? Truly a question of importance. So it is finally for their degree of harmony with Exodus 12 and with each other, though it is initially for their own sake, that Isaiah 53 and Psalms 41.9 now have our interest.

A number of verses from Isaiah 53 are fulfilled, sometimes to our great satisfaction, sometimes not. Among them are:

53.3–8 despised and rejected of men . . . taken from prison ("Whether of the twain will ye . . . Barabbas," Mt 27.15–21, cf. Mk 15.6–11, Lk 23.18, Jn 18.39–40, Acts 3.14)

53.4 he hath borne our griefs, and carried our sorrows ("spoken by Esaias the prophet, saying, himself took our infirmities, and bare our sicknesses," Mt 8.17; Stendahl *School of Matthew* 2nd ed. pp. 106–107 sees that the Isaiah verse as here quoted follows the Septuagint, which has given the Hebrew a "spiritualized interpretation," and that the gospel version—bypassing the Septuagint—may have been translated from the Hebrew by the evangelist himself)

53.9 with the rich in his death ("there came a rich man of Arimathaea," Mt 27.57)

53.12 he was numbered with the transgressors ("with him they crucify two thieves . . . And the scripture was fulfilled, which saith, And he was numbered with the transgressors," Mk 15.27–28, cf. Mt 27.38, Lk 22.37, 23.32)

53.12 made intercession for the transgressors ("Then said Jesus, Father, forgive them," Lk 23.34)

Being a rosary of paratactic components, rather than a cluster of syntactic ones, the passage—like all Hebrew poetry—is memorable versewise, not as a whole; and it has been fulfilled similarly. The transgressors Jesus was numbered among were the malefactors, but the transgressors he made intercession for were the people, the rulers, and the soldiers. Nor can it have been truly said of him that—in fulfilment of another verse from the chapter—"he shall see his seed, he shall prolong his days . . . and he shall divide the spoil with the strong."

The verses I have cited from Isaiah 53 all seem to be secondary. What verse was the primary one, conveying these others? For the fourth gospel it was 53.12 with 53.7 "brought as a lamb to the slaughter . . . he bare the sin of many" ("the Lamb of God, which taketh away the sin of the world," Jn 1.29). For the synoptic gospels it was simply 53.12 "he bare the sin of many" ("which is shed for many for the remission of sins," Mt 26.28, cf. Mk 14.24, Lk 22.20, 1 Cor. 11.24). And behind this verse—"he bare the sin of many"—stands the name of Jesus "the Lord is salvation," interpreted as saying that "he shall save his people from their sins" (Mt 1.21, cf. Acts 4.12, 10.43).

Psalms 41.9–10—"Yea, mine own familiar friend, in whom I trusted, which did eat of my bread, hath lifted up his heel against me. But thou, O Lord, be merciful unto me, and raise me up, that I may requite them"—has three matters in common with the gospels: the eating of bread, the betrayal, and the resurrection. But again the passage is fulfilled selectively: Jesus has nothing to do with the earlier verse "I said, Lord, be merciful unto me: heal my soul; for I have sinned against thee." Among the eating of bread, the betrayal, and the resurrection, which is responsible for the others? Not the last: "raise me up" as a prophecy of the resurrection would be obscure, even though the word qûm recurs in Hosea 6.2 "in the third day he will raise us up"; and the simple sense of "that I may requite them" would be unsuitable. The choice for the primary element, which the other elements are secondary to, is between the eating of bread and the betrayal. The older of these must be the eating of bread, for Jesus and his disciples will have shared meals from the beginning; the betrayal is less necessary, for Jesus did not hide and could always be found. So the eating of bread with Jesus, and afterwards in his memory, caused his followers to believe that, in fulfilment of Psalms 41.9, he had been betrayed (the thirty pieces of silver, the potter, and the treasury were then remembered from Zechariah 11.13).

How well did the fulfilments—of things "written in the law of Moses, and in the prophets, and in the psalms"—combine with each other? One thing was the passover, Exodus 12, fulfilled by Jesus as the passover lamb in the fourth gospel, and as the passover bread in the synoptic gospels. Another thing was Isaiah 53.7–12 "a lamb to the slaughter . . . he bare the sin of many," fulfilled by "the Lamb of God, which taketh away the sin of the world" in the fourth gospel; or else it was simply 53.12 "he bare the sin of many," fulfilled by "which is shed for many for the remission of sins" in the synoptic gospels. Yet another thing was the betrayal by one who shared bread, in Psalms 41.9, fulfilled in all the gospels, with different degrees of elaboration. Were the fulfilments compatible or at odds with each other?

The problem is more complicated than I have allowed. For there were other influences. The phrases "blood of the covenant" (Ex. 24.8) and "make a new covenant" (Jer. 31.31) combined into "blood of the new testament" (Mt 26.28, Mk 14.24, Lk 22.20, cf. 1 Cor. 10.16), and the resemblance of blood to wine ("he washed his garments in wine, and his clothes in the blood of grapes," Gen. 49.11; "the pure blood of the grape," Deut. 32.14) suggested that the blood might figuratively be drunk. And yet other sources or analogues may easily be found. Still, our inferences—about whether the fulfilments mesh well or badly—will be valid; and they are as follows (the former summary having to do with John, the latter with Matthew, Mark, and Luke):

> The passover lamb (Ex. 12.21) and "a lamb to the slaughter" (Isa. 53.7) are one and the same by nature; both are fulfilled in Jesus as the lamb; this emblem does though impede his being also the bread and the wine. That he should be betrayed by one who ate of his bread (Ps. 41.9) is neither impeded nor furthered, for the lamb emblem and the betrayal at bread neither repel nor attract each other.

> When Jesus is seen as the passover bread (of Ex. 12.17) he is not also seen as the lamb; the bread emblem does though combine well with one of wine as blood, the two elements suggesting each other; and the bread is broken as the body will be torn, the wine being shared as the blood will be shed for many (so Isa. 53.12). The bread emblem also combines inevitably with the betrayal at bread (Ps. 41.9).

It is a structural flaw in the synoptic gospels that the one bread becomes the other. The fourth gospel—though nonnaturalistic, for the disciples seem paralyzed—has no such flaw inherent. In Matthew particularly, but also in Mark and even in Luke, we are appalled by the realization that Judas partakes of the bread and the wine, which Jesus gives as his body and as his blood for the remission of sins. Should not the elements bring him spiritual nourishment and lead him to repent of the sin he has in mind?

3. A third other era: the time of waiting

The third affinity of the last supper with matters of another era is from 1 Corinthians 11.24–26. The words "in remembrance of me" (spoken by Jesus)—and "For as often as ye eat this bread, and drink this cup, ye do shew the Lord's death till he come" (written by

Paul)—imply a continuity between the "this is my body" ceremony at the last supper and its reenactment. The "in remembrance of me" occurs in the gospels only in Luke 22.19b–20, a disputed passage which Green (ed. *Matthew* on Mt 26.26–29) would print, believing that what Jesus said at the last supper was "naturally preserved and handed on" in two traditions: the one, Mark followed by Matthew; the other, Paul and independently Luke. Westcott and Hort reject Luke 22.19b–20, however, noting that the verses are not in the Western documents, and thinking that valued words are more often borrowed than lost. Tasker (ed. the Greek text for the New English Bible) notes besides that 22.19b–20 is not in the Lukan style. And there is another consideration, to my mind the most telling. Neither Jesus nor the evangelists who narrated his life would have looked beyond the resurrection into a time of waiting for the second coming, whereas Paul—minded less upon the life of Jesus than upon the resurrection and the waiting—would have found the "in remembrance" most fitting. It is not a question of who wrote the later, Paul or the evangelists, but of who wrote from the later perspective; and it was Paul who did. So I take Luke 22.19b–20, with its phrase "in remembrance of me," to have been copied from 1 Corinthians 11.24–25 by some redactor. I then take the words of Jesus, as they are given in 1 Corinthians 11.24–25, to have been impenetrated, and amplified, by the thought of the writer.

There are accordingly several considerations that lead to the same conclusion:

1. In the fourth gospel Jesus is the passover lamb which taketh away the sin of the world; in the synoptic gospels he is the passover bread and the disciples are bidden to eat of his body; the narratives of the last supper, conforming to these different symbols, cannot be harmonized.

2. The etymological typology of *pascha* would account, as no other factor would, for the twofold sense in which Jesus, about to die, is the passover.

3. In the book of Acts the feast of unleavened bread is observed without mention of Jesus.

4. In the *Didache* a thanksgiving or "eucharist" is described: a blessing over wine and bread, in the name of Jesus, but without allusion to the last supper.

5. The words "in remembrance of me" were added by Paul to the narrative of the last supper that had come to him.

The conclusion led to by these considerations is that the sacrament commemorating the last supper was not continuous with, but was a good number of years later than, the supper itself. The conclusion does not follow for certain, and to me it is not desirable; but I believe it to be probable.

When did Paul add the "in remembrance" to the last supper? Perhaps at the earlier time he now refers to. "For I have received of the Lord that which also I delivered unto you, That the Lord Jesus the same night in which he was betrayed took bread" (1 Cor. 11.23). The sense is difficult: does "received of the Lord" mean "received from heaven"? does *delivered* anticipate *betrayed*, seeing that in Greek they are forms of the same word? and was it orally that the delivery was made? Whatever the answers, the prior teaching—referred to in the phrase "which also I delivered unto you"—was ineffectual, and so need not be looked into. I would accordingly credit the "in remembrance" to the present moment, when the epistle is being written. And what is true for the words is true for the thought. The last supper becomes a rite in this very chapter. The baffling relationship between a hunger-satisfying meal and a ceremony can accordingly be understood. Paul is changing the one into the other, or adding to the one an aspect of the other. The chapter preceding might be a stumblingblock in my path, though. "The cup of blessing which we bless, is it not the communion of the blood of Christ? The bread which we break, is it not the communion of the body of Christ?" (10.16). If these rhetorical questions rephrase what was already a general confession of faith, the remembrance of the last supper had already been instituted, and was not about to *become* instituted in the words following (11.24–26). I assume, though, that in the rhetorical questions (10.16) the apostle is saying something interesting, rather than what everybody knows. If he is, then the cup blessed and the bread broken—blessed and broken by Christians at their common meals—have not until now been thought of as the blood and the body. It follows that the 10th and 11th chapters of 1 Corinthians are the origin of the liturgy.

What awareness led Paul to add the "in remembrance"? In the earliest surviving Christian writing there is mention

> of anxiety that some believers are dying before the End has come. This was apparently a shock, for it had been expected that believers would not die (1 Thessalonians 4.13–18). In Mark (9.1) Jesus is represented as slightly modifying that expectation: "There are some standing here who will not taste death before they see the kingdom of God come with power." Much later, in 2 Peter 3.4 we hear of scoffers who say "Where is the promise of his coming?" why is nothing changing, why is the world just as it has always been? These passages and many others (e.g., Matthew 10.23; 1 Corinthians 7.29, 31; 10.11; Romans 13.11) point irresistibly to the conclusion that the Baptist, Jesus, and Jesus' first followers expected the End very soon. (Cupitt *The Debate about Christ* p. 68)

The second coming had been delayed, and the crisis was the greater if one thought that all promises had been kept. What was the use of forehappening and recurrence—what did it matter that Jesus was the second Adam, the second Moses, the second Joshua, the second Jonah—if years were to continue the same as before? Where lay the value in the pattern if its completion made no difference? To answer, Paul needed a new theology, one that would regard Jesus less as the final than as the central event.

"For as often as ye eat this bread, and drink this cup, ye do shew the Lord's death till he come" (1 Cor. 11.26). Until now, the two sources of type and antitype had been the old covenant and the new, or else the earthly kingdom and the heavenly. Here for the first time they were the life of Jesus and its reenactment. The interim between the resurrection and the second coming was no longer meaningless. The last supper—in typology—had become no longer an antitype looking backwards upon the passover, nor any longer a type looking forwards to a Messianic feast in the next world; it had become a type looking forwards to perpetual renewal while this world should last.

That the betrayer partook of the bread and the wine, after they had been said to be the body and the blood, was a dreadful thought from the synoptic gospels. In 1 Corinthians 11 it is brought into the grand scheme of things, as one who eats the bread and drinks the cup of the Lord unworthily is said to be liable for the body and the blood of the Lord (verse 27). None of the church fathers speaks of this type and antitype, the traitor at the last supper and the unworthy lot at the reenactments; but I think all the same that the apostle made the comparison. The typology is both positive and negative, governing both the good and the bad among the disciples, and among those who partake of the sacraments.

Paul can now see why some from the Christian community are dying before the second coming: those who eat and drink (at the communal meals or rites), without discerning the Lord's body, eat and drink judgment upon themselves (verse 29); this is why many are sick and several dead. It was an idea for an age when physical and spiritual health were thought allied. And it sounds fine today in the exhortation from the Book of Common Prayer: receiving the sacraments unworthily

> we eat and drink our own damnation, not considering the Lord's
> Body; we kindle God's wrath against us; we provoke him to plague
> us with divers diseases, and sundry kinds of death.

This expressly to the people of Corinth. Not everyone is mindful of Jesus at the fellowship meals. Some are boisterous, reckless; some—sick or even dead—have already been punished for being so.

Paul is sometimes difficult to understand (2 Pet. 3.16), but what he says is usually apt. Are the words "Christ our passover" in 1 Corinthians 5.7 pertinent to the incest which that chapter began by speaking of? Yes, they are. The Corinthians are puffed up like leavened bread; it would be better if they resembled Jesus, the unleavened passover. Why are they puffed up? They take glory in the celebrity of their hero Oedipus, who was prophesied to lie with his mother, Merope, wife of Polybus, king of Corinth. The apostle has not heard the whole story, as with the paradox about Epimenides (Titus 1.12); but his verses make sense, and are not nonsequiturs.

I would similarly defend the "in remembrance" and "For as often . . . till he come" in 1 Corinthians 11.24–26, which Richardson *Mass and Lord's Supper* p. 598 holds to be not Pauline, but a later addition. True, Paul is not interested elsewhere either in ritual or in what Jesus did during his lifetime. Still, the words seem authentic because of their relevancy. On the night he was betrayed, Jesus had a last supper with his disciples. Those who afterwards behave unworthily at a supper of his followers, and do not discern him in the bread and wine, betray him anew. It can be seen who they are, for some are sick and some dead. A typology for the era following the resurrection—devised here and now in this chapter of this letter—tells why not everyone, among the Christians, is living until the second coming. The phrases "in remembrance" and "For as often . . . till he come" are so much at home in their context that we should have missed them if they had been wanting.

What is the connection between the last supper and the death of Jesus? In the synoptic gospels at the supper the death is foreseen; the body and the blood are sacrificed in anticipation. Is it true then that according to 1 Corinthians the body and the blood are sacrificed at the reenactment? Schweitzer *Paul and his Interpreters* pp. 198–199 thinks not: what one eats and drinks are the bread and the cup. Our argument from typology would lead us to disagree. It is more than the bread and the cup—to Paul—at the communion or remembrance. For if those who unworthily eat the bread and drink the cup are liable for Jesus' death, then those who *worthily* partake must renew the role of the faithful disciples. The worthy communicant, as an antitype of Peter or Matthew or James the Less, hears the words "this is my body . . . this is my blood."

D. Is the Lord's supper compatible with modern science?

Biblical cosmology takes the earth to be the hub of things; the sun rises as a light by day, the stars follow courses by night. The cosmology of *Heraclides* or *Copernicus*—heeding diagrams and equations rather than the impression of the senses—denies that the sun rises: the earth is a sphere that spins on its axis towards the sun and away from it (whence day and night), and also encircles the sun (whence the seasons). *Modern* cosmology—strange to the common man, hardly within his grasp—holds that the gravitational tug on the earth is the curvature of the spacetime continuum in the neighbourhood of a mass (see Gamow in *Scientific American* Sept. 1956 p. 139). Most of those who write about the existence of God have a biblical, not many have a Copernican viewpoint. None (unless I am mistaken) has a modern viewpoint. What follows then is my own attempt. I have no right to the subject except that it interests me more perhaps than any other. Nor would I speak about it here, were not the preceding essays, freethinking as they are, liable to be thought unChristian and even atheistical.

God is that Law which governs matter and energy. Before our universe began, matter and energy—and gravity and electromagnetism—were perhaps different than they are now; the Law was the same; and so for the era after our universe has ended. If the matryoschka dolls are numerous without limit, some larger than a galaxy, some smaller than a quark, the Law controls them all. Terms from a catechism come to mind: infinite, immutable, eternal, incomprehensible, almighty, most absolute.

The definition I have offered is a physical, not a metaphysical one. The symbols that would best express it belong to mathematics, not to language. Construct a circle, with a centre at zero horizontally and zero vertically. Say that the east and west are the square roots of one; the north and south, those of minus one. Now locate the three cube roots of one. The obvious solution is the number itself. What are the other solutions? Find them by constructing an equilateral triangle as shown. The points drawn are soon figured to be the sums $(-1 + \sqrt{-3})/2$ and $(-1 - \sqrt{-3})/2$. Call

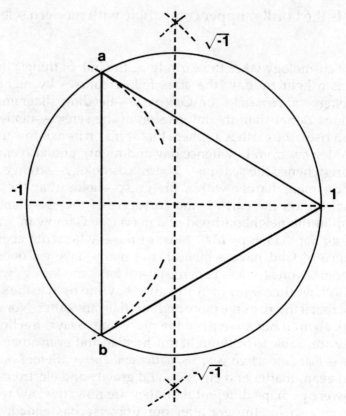

these a and b. See that $a^2 = b$ and $b^2 = a$, so that $a^3 = b^3 = ab = 1$. How beautiful this is! what a cause for wonder! Who would have thought that the square root of minus three could play a role in a cube root of one? Elsewhere paragraphs of words may be the suitable mode of expression, but here arrays of quantities are the more suitable. Similarly for a description of God. Until now, language alone has, algebra and geometry have not, claimed to approach him. But the summa theologica for our age will be a unified field theory. Say though that the primal forces never appear wholly compatible with each other. To that degree, the Law will be unknowable, inexpressible, deeper than our fathoming. The best probe will still be the abstractions of mathematics.

Why is there something rather than nothing? Matter may prevail over antimatter owing to some deep asymmetry (see Hinds in *American Scientist* 69:430–436). Why then should matter have come to exist in the first place? Because a universe of energy but no matter may be unstable (see Wilczek in *Scientific American* Dec. 1980 p. 90). Why though is there a certain moderate amount of matter and energy, rather than either a zero or an endless amount? Truly there would be a higher order of mathematical elegance in either nullity or plenitude. It looks as if matter and energy are imperfect in comparison with, say, prumblag and swidvoth.

Consider now Anselm's proof for the existence of God: "Conceive of a being greater than which nothing else can be conceived of; acknowledge that to exist in reality as well as in the mind is greater than to exist in the mind alone; conclude that the supreme being must accordingly exist in reality." This argument fails so long as our world exists: the mole in the gemstone is the finitude of matter and energy. The middle step cannot be taken if it means that to exist along with limited things is in all ways greater than to escape limitation by not existing. The first step even tells against the author's intention. For the greatest being we can conceive of fills the categories of matter and energy, as well as those of space and time, and thereby entirely displaces ourselves. There is perhaps a reason why such a being could not exist. But we are able to *conceive* of its existing, and our doing so turns the demonstration awry.

A refutation of my definition might be: "If God is noncontingent, and if the Law governing finite packets of matter and energy is contingent by virtue of ruling over contingent subjects, then God is not the Law." In reply I would deny the minor premise if possible, but deny the major if need be. Is the unchanging Law contingent in consequence of its rule over finite quantities? On the condition that the answer is yes, I allow that God is contingent also. What I disallow is that God does not exist. In this respect my definition resembles the Tetragrammaton, rendered "I am who am" or "I am that I am": a reaffirmation of being; for how can one say that *What is* is not? Instead of postulating the perfection and then inquiring into the existence of God, I postulate the existence and leave the question of perfection to the philosophers.

The theology I have sketched magnifies God as much as the

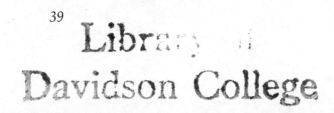
Library
Davidson College

theology of yore did. It gives no comfort to the brokenhearted, though, and allows the scoundrel to escape; there is neither consolation nor retribution. And as the Law does not answer us, so is it not answerable to us. Still, a man may have such well-being that he seems to be like a son of God. Is he then as we are, and not rather of a superior tribe? I will say that he is the perfect member of our own tribe, such as has existed perhaps once. Certain aspects of character are inborn (see Holden in *Science* 207:1323–1328); and the figure I have been speaking of shall be thought to have a *dynamis*, or force, not as a violation of nature but as a singularity, an element in his DNA code if you will; and say further that the effects of this trait are felt by all who see him or touch him. I have been present at a working of wonders, and do not distrust the priest who wrought them (Ralph DiOrio: see the Lansing *State Journal*, 28 March 1981); they may have been furthered by group hysteria, but they owed something to the magnetism of the healer. What if the charisma were a thousandfold greater? Strange, unique things can be done, or can have been done, by the physician whose will is overwhelming. How are you to get rid of warts? The most effective medicine is to be told, by one who has never known his method to fail, that you should put on this brown liquid dropwise every day, and they will be gone in a week (see Thomas *The Medusa and the Snail*, pp. 76–81). Why should not leprosy be cured similarly, even at once, by a yet more powerful magus, one whose rapport with God is intimate? My portrait of Jesus, putting him on earth but making him not of common stuff, may be retouched as you like. I have only laid a basis in biology for a life that justifies more than admiration alone.

What do we know about Jesus? We know that he lived; that Socrates lived is no more certain. What else do we know about him? That to those in his coterie he was nonpareil. All that remains must be sifted. The practice of ancient authors was to heighten their matter; a Thucydides on the first crusade would have let us hear the rallying speech of Urban II. If the evangelist had thought that his narrative would be better with such and such a detail, he would not have been reluctant to add it. We are then excused from believing in the gospels as chronicles. This is pleasing and may strengthen faith. For the happenings—a walking on the water, a changing of water into wine—are not so grand as our own walking on the moon, or changing of one creature into another by genetic engineering. Better that the stories about Jesus should be regarded as attempts to keep for ever a life more worthy of being kept than any other. Better too that there should be mystery and bewilderment, in harmony with our understanding of the physical world.

Of the two paths to God, the one is through study. We have looked with Faustian vision when we see why a jellyfish has the shape of a splash made by a pebble, or see why there are (except for viruses, bacteria, and blue-green algae) thirteen subunits to every microtubule in every cell of every living thing, or see how in intergalactic space five objects can be equidistant from each other (Callahan in *Scientific American* Aug. 1976 p. 92). The other path to God is through spiritual ecstasy. If we contemplate Jesus in our devotions, it ought to be with awe, though at times with a sense of oneness. Some prefer sermons and asceticism; others, snake-handling and a speaking in tongues. I myself would have the sacrament before all else. For me, the trappings and vessels shall be incense, mosaics, and such wording as the Authorized Version is couched in. Not that everything must belong to an earlier time: Dali's "Corpus Hypercubus" has powerful spirituality. To me, the articles of faith should be taken figuratively; but differences are wholesome: if "the chief end of man is to glorify God, and to enjoy him forever," as the Presbyterians have it, then one will decide for oneself just how the life of Jesus is a means to that end.

II. Does the *Inferno* have one higher sense, or three, or none?

A. Aquinas and the letter to Cangrande

In his *Summa Theologica* (first part, question 1, article 10), Aquinas acknowledges that Augustine (Migne *PL* 42.68; see Moore *Studies in Dante* 3rd ser. p. 309) classified the senses of scripture as the historical, the etiological, the analogical, and the allegorical (and allows that besides these there is the parabolical). He himself would classify the senses as the literal (or historical), the allegorical, the moral (or tropological), and the anagogical. Are not the lists incompatible? Aquinas explains that now the primary sense, now the spiritual one, has been subdivided. The schemes may accordingly be outlined: Augustine on the left, Aquinas on the right:

1. the literal sense	1. the literal (historical) sense
a. the historical	2. the allegorical sense
b. the etiological	a. the allegorical
c. the analogical	b. the moral (tropological)
(the parabolical)	c. the anagogical
2. the allegorical sense	

That the meaning of "allegorical" and of "historical" should be now broad or generic, now narrow or specific, is a minor flaw that remains. What Aquinas wishes to denote as the three spiritual senses, or the three aspects of the spiritual sense, is put clearly enough: *allegorical* (in its narrow meaning) is when the things of the Old Law signify those of the New; *moral* is when the things done in Christ, or the things that signify Christ, are signs for what we ought to do; *anagogical* is when the things of eternal glory are signified. Let us accept these demarcations, hoping that they may be useful. (And let us, to avoid ambiguity, sometimes supplement "allegorical," in its narrow meaning, with "typological.")

In the *Convivio* (2nd tractate, first section)—a middle work between the *Vita Nuova* and the *Commedia*—Dante first says that his commentary will be both literal and allegorical. He then names as the senses that writings may have: the literal, the allegorical, the moral, and the anagogical:

> When Ovid tells that Orpheus tamed the beasts with his lyre, and drew the trees and stones towards himself, the allegorical sense is that a wise man uses the music of his voice to make cruel hearts mild, and to move those who do not have the liberal arts. When the gospel tells that Christ, ascending the mountain for the transfiguration, took only a few of his disciples with him, the moral sense is that for secret affairs we should have few companions. And when, in the song of the prophet, Israel went out of Egypt, and Judea was made free, the anagogical sense is that as the soul departs from sin she is made free and holy. (condensed)

Aquinas is being followed, but with freewheeling. The word "allegorical" has a specific meaning only, not a generic one as well. Nor does it still speak of scripture only, nor even of sacred writings only, but now refers to secular lore just as readily. The allegorical (typological) sense no longer relates the old law to the new, but has become a moral sense without Christ. Dante admits that theologians use the word differently; he prefers for himself the usage of poets. We could ask many questions, for a great deal remains obscure. Are two of the spiritual senses—are all three of them— ever to be found together?

In section 7 of the letter to Cangrande—written after, and about, the *Commedia*—Dante describes his poem as polysemous "having many meanings," and again speaks first of just literal and allegorical (or mystical) senses, but then of literal, allegorical, moral, and anagogical ones. As if borrowing from the *Convivio*, he chooses for illustration Psalms 114.1 (113.1), a verse more heavily pregnant than any other: "When Israel went out of Egypt, the house of Jacob from a people of strange language":

. . . if we consider the letter alone, the thing signified to us is the going out of the children of Israel from Egypt in the time of Moses; if the allegory, our redemption through Christ is signified; if the moral sense, the conversion of the soul from the sorrow and misery of sin to a state of grace is signified; if the anagogical, the passing of the sanctified soul from the bondage of the corruption of this world to the liberty of everlasting glory is signified. And although these mystical meanings are called by various names, they may one and all in a general sense be termed allegorical. . . . (Toynbee trans.)

Aquinas is here imitated closely. The meaning of "allegorical" is at one moment narrow; at another, broad. All three spiritual senses belong, to judge from the example, to scripture only, or to other sacred writings as well, but not to secular ones. The allegory of the poets has been abandoned. What is the source of the interpretation? Without looking hard I see three good analogues: Augustine (Migne *PL* 42.70) on Paul's comment (1 Cor. 10.1–11) upon the exodus, which identifies Moses as Christ (the allegorical = typological sense); Rabanus Maurus (Migne *PL* 112.919) on "When Israel went out of Egypt" as meaning that the elect recognize their sins and depart from them (the moral sense); and Gregory Nazianzenus (Migne *PG* 36.636) on the passover as telling not only of a historical event but also of our ascent from earthly things into those beyond (the anagogical sense). Or perhaps Dante had no source at all, but merely interpreted by the fashion prevailing. That he has now found all the spiritual senses in the same verse is very satisfying.

Can it be that these three higher senses match the divisions of the *Commedia*? From grace to glory (anagogical) would answer to the *Paradiso*; from sin to grace (moral), to the *Purgatorio*. But redemption through Christ (allegorical) would not answer to the *Inferno*. So the "When Israel" verse has only affinity, not wholesale correspondence, with the *Commedia*.

In section 8 of the Cangrande letter, Dante uses "allegorical" in its broad meaning, as if not to claim for the poem great complexity, after all. The subject of the whole work he says to be, in the literal sense, "the state of souls after death," and in the allegorical sense "man according as by his merits or demerits in the exercise of his free will he is deserving of reward or punishment by justice" (Toynbee trans.). Does "allegorical" here mean allegorical (typological), or moral, or anagogical? or does it have yet another meaning? I believe it means moral; it does not mean allegorical (typological); it might mean anagogical. The phrase "man . . . deserving of reward or punishment" could even be taken for the literal sense. But, however we decide, that the *Commedia* has three higher senses, and not one only, no longer seems so likely as it did. We would now say that sections 7 and 8 disagree with each other, that neither agrees with the *Convivio*, and that neither summarizes what the poet has done. The inconsistency is the most troublesome one in Dante. For this reason and others—see Brugnoli in the *Opere minori* vol. 2 pp. 512–521—many have regarded the Cangrande letter as spurious, at least in part. I would not belligerently claim it to be genuine; I would only see whether section 7 may not help us to say what principles the poem is constructed by. Which of the higher senses is the most authentic, which has the best precedent in the bible itself?

B. The principal higher sense of scripture

The *literal* sense of "When Israel went out of Egypt, the house of Jacob from a people of strange language" is given in section 7 of the letter as "the departure of the children of Israel from Egypt in the time of Moses." Israel and Jacob are synonymous names (recurring in the Old Testament as a formulaic word pair); so "the children of Israel" is a fusion of "Israel" with "the house of Jacob"; Dante has made two into one, turned poetry into prose. The circumlocution "people of strange language," synonymous with "Egypt" and completing the parallelism, has been omitted from the interpretation; but again the change is not one of substance. Where in the psalm is there a reference to Moses? His presence is implied, though scarcely; if he was looked for, then he could be found: that is all. The lesson for readers is, the literal sense of a passage may contain matter unexpressed.

The *allegorical* sense of "When Israel went out of Egypt" is given as "our redemption through Christ." Israel corresponds to ourselves, humanity under grace; the exodus corresponds to redemption. Where is the analogue to Christ? Aquinas said that the sense was allegorical (typological) when the things of the Old Law signified those of the New. Who or what then is it that signifies Christ? Moses, unmentioned though he is. Christ is the antitype, Moses the type; the copy surpasses the rough sketch or blueprint. What was the origin of typology, the study of prefiguration, of forehappening and recurrence? was it Judaic or Hellenistic? The first announcement of it can be credited to Jesus himself:

> But he answered and said unto them, An evil and adulterous generation seeketh after a sign; and there shall no sign be given to it, but the sign of the prophet Jonah: For as Jonah was three days and three nights in the whale's belly, so shall the Son of man be three days and three nights in the heart of the earth. (Mt 12.39–40)

Fanciful, no doubt; a conundrum. Must we blame the teacher for it? No; we may blame the disciple, the evangelist, instead. The early Christians retold, rather than rewrote, the sayings of their master, and changed them (since oral transmission is fluid). The beginnings of typology were in the times, in the years just preceding or just following the crucifixion; that is all we can say for certain. Perhaps the machine was put into motion by Paul, a legalist whom it would aid mightily:

> . . . after the similitude of Adam's transgression, who is the figure of him that was to come. (Rom. 5.14)

Christ is the antitype; Adam here is the type; Jonah elsewhere is another type; Moses in Psalms 114.1 (113.1), by the Cangrande letter, is yet another; Isaac and Joshua are, or were to the church fathers, types par excellence. And there are antitypes of other types:

46

And from the days of John the Baptist until now the kingdom of heaven suffereth violence, and the violent take it by force. For all the prophets and the law prophesied until John. And if ye will receive it, this is Elijah, which was for to come. He that hath ears to hear, let him hear. (Mt 11.12–15, cf. Malachi 4.5)

One person or place or item is compared or equated with another; the type is historical; the antitype is historical, too; the likeness or bond between them—between Elijah and John the Baptist—is inexplicable, mystical.

The *moral* sense of "When Israel went out of Egypt" is "the conversion of the soul from the sorrow and misery of sin to a state of grace." We are skeptical for two reasons. First, the movement is no longer at least partly from concrete to concrete as with typology (Moses foreshadowing Christ), but is now wholly from concrete to abstract. Secondly—whereas we have been bidden (if not by him in whom there was no guile, then at least by the evangelist) to see certain types, or signs or figures, and their antitypes—we have not been bidden by any biblical directive to see a moral sense. (It is true that there are parables in both Testaments: Nathan judged David with one. The literal, primary sense of a parable, though, is not to be taken from its fable alone, but from its lesson as well, since the fable exists for the sake of the lesson; Aquinas was right in saying that the literal sense included the parabolical. The literal, primary sense of "When Israel went out of Egypt," on the other hand, is historical, and the lesson offered to us, through the interpretation, is secondary, additional.) Still, Augustine—and hence Aquinas, and hence Dante—did have for the moral sense an ancient authority. For just when typology was being applied to the Old Testament by Paul, moral allegorizing was being applied to it by Philo:

. . . one would expect, when a tyrant dies, those over whom he has tyrannized to be glad and rejoice; yet it is then that they are said to lament, for we are told "after those many days the king of Egypt died, and the children of Israel lamented sorely" (Ex. 2.23). Taken literally the sentence is contradictory to reason. If it apply to the powers that sway the soul, the statement of the second clause is

47

seen to be consequent upon that in the first. Pharaoh is the power that scatters to the winds and flings away all ideas of what is noble. When this power is quick and active in us and seems to be strong and healthy, if indeed any evil power may be said to be healthy, we drive self-control far from us, and welcome pleasure. But, when the author of our foul and licentious life weakens and, so to speak, dies, we are brought all at once to a clear view of the life of self-mastery, and turn to lamenting and bewailing ourselves for our old mode of living, seeing that, preferring pleasure to virtue, we overlaid immortal with mortal life. ("The Worse Attacks the Better" 94–95, Colson and Whitaker trans., Loeb Philo vol. 2)

The *anagogical* "upwards leading" sense of the "When Israel" verse is "the passing of the sanctified soul from the bondage of the corruption of this world to the liberty of everlasting glory." This fourth sense does not have the celebrity belonging to the allegorical (typological) sense or to the moral sense. Only one biblical passage, and no other authority, seems to lie behind it; here "allegory" is used in its broad meaning:

Abraham had two sons, the one by a bondmaid, the other by a freewoman. But he who was of the bondwoman was born after the flesh; but he of the freewoman was by promise. Which things are an allegory: for these are the two covenants; the one from the mount Sinai, which gendereth to bondage, which is Hagar. For this Hagar is mount Sinai in Arabia, and answereth to Jerusalem which now is, and is in bondage with her children. But Jerusalem which is above is free, which is the mother of us all. (Gal. 4.22–25)

The anagogical element—there are other elements—is the two cities of Jerusalem, the one earthly, the other heavenly. So: the anagogical and the moral sense are scarcely warranted by scripture; the allegorical (typological) sense is more important by far; the literal sense is supreme. What we wish to know is whether the same will be true for Dante.

C. A literal-anagogical continuum in the *Inferno*

Is there at least one of the higher senses in every canto? Neither the *Summa Theologica* nor the letter to Cangrande said that every chapter of the Psalms or Genesis or the gospels—let alone every verse—had more senses than the literal one alone. The fourfold complex was—convincingly or not—discovered in Psalms 114.1 (113.1), but examples tend to be good ones, not typical ones. We have no directive to see a fourfold or even a threefold or twofold meaning throughout scripture. Still less do we have such a directive for the *Commedia*.

The *allegorical* (typological) sense plays its role either when elements of the Old Testament prefigure those of the New, or when those of the New look backwards upon those of the Old. May not elements from our own time also be types? The early Christians thought that soon all would be fulfilled and then the world would end. A dozen centuries later, the life and death of Christ seemed to be not the closing act, but the central one. The last supper had become not the final passover, but a ceremony to be renewed perpetually. So persons and events from Troy or Rome or Florence, from ancient times or modern, may be types mirroring, highlighting, those of the gospel. We need merely to take the antitype for perfection; it can occur before the type as well as after. How many items in the *Commedia* have an allegorical (typological) sense glimmeringly? how many do so with the brightness of noon? I will look for the types most searchingly at the climaxes, the great heights and depths.

The *moral* sense may be thought to lie in what Bergin (*Dante* p. 216) calls "the moral system" of hell, purgatory, and paradise. An earthly life has as background a locale in the world to come. Here are the avaricious; the violent against God are over there, yet closer to the core of hell; the hypocrites are closer still. Or: this is the place of avarice; that, the place of violence against God; that place yonder is the one of hypocrisy. The arrangement is architectural and absolute. The moral sense does not always have immediacy, but it is undisguised and never in doubt. Lead the life of so and so, with this or that badness or goodness; then as punishment or reward have such and such a habitation after death, with its harsh or pleasant climate.

The *anagogical* sense may be taken from the words "what I was living, that am I dead" (*Inf.* 14.51). Our earthly life is a foreshadow of the one to follow, or, the life that follows is a completion—or *extension*—of the one here. If there were value in terminology, it would often be better to speak of the catagogical or the apagogical sense. We must at any rate conceive of negative anagogy—not a leading towards, but a leading from, paradise or purgatory or hell. Really, the direction (time forwards to eternity, or eternity backwards to time) is an unimportant, scholastic issue. What matters is that the two sorts of existence may furnish two senses of the poem. As the "Jerusalem which now is" answers to the "Jerusalem which is above," the Brunetto in hell answers—in an anagogical sense—to the Brunetto who lived amongst us.

Whether much of scripture has the higher senses is moot, at least so far as we see today. What then about the *Commedia*? Its allegorical (typological), moral, and anagogical senses are likely to be more pronounced than those of scripture, as having been more earnestly intended. The letter to Cangrande, though it does not further biblical study, will perhaps be helpful for the *Inferno*. A danger is that we may say the same thing in four different ways. To skirt redundancy, let us compare one sense with another. There will be caution in doing so, and novelty as well.

The allegorical (typological) and moral senses are discrete. The literal and anagogical senses are allied to each other. Some of the souls so closely resemble their historical persons, in fact, that we conceive of a literal-anagogical continuum. Here lies a problem: are the literal and anagogical senses really two? would they not better be regarded as one? An argument by Auerbach implies strongly that they are two. To his mind, the model for the literal-anagogical relationship lay in biblical typology, or figurism:

> Cato is a *figura*, or rather the earthly Cato, who renounced his life for freedom, was a *figura*, and the Cato who appears here in the

Purgatorio is the revealed or fulfilled figure, the truth of that figural event. (*Scenes* pp. 65–66)

Thus Virgil in the *Divine Comedy* is the historical Virgil himself, but then again he is not; for the historical Virgil is only a *figura* of the fulfilled truth that the poem reveals, and this fulfillment is more real, more significant than the *figura*. (*Scenes* p. 71)

These words—which Auerbach later restated (*Mimesis* p. 195)—are not simply untrue, but they are not simply true, either. For figurism, or typology, sees one person or event as fulfilled in another, *different* person or event. In scripture, and in the church fathers, those who are likened to or identified with each other, in a mystical fashion, are historically distinct, never the same. Accordingly, Jonah . . . Christ, or Adam . . . Christ, or Moses . . . Christ, or Elijah . . . John the Baptist, would not have suggested Cato . . . Cato or Virgil . . . Virgil.

Consider the literal-anagogical continuum in the 11th book of the *Odyssey*. The shades of Agamemnon and Achilles address Odysseus, a pilgrim in their realm, as "Zeus-born Laertiades, Odysseus of many arts" (403, 473), just as they had done when living (*Il.* 4.358, 9.308); and he addresses them as "Atreides, most glorious, king of men Agamemnon" (397) and "O Achilles, son of Peleus, by far the mightiest of the Achaeans" (478), also just as when they were living (*Il.* 9.677, 19.210). Earthly protocols lie in these full-line titles, customs continued among the ghosts. And in other ways too the comrades are like their old selves. As Agamemnon was by natural right the first to be named among the quick (*Il.* 3.167–170), so is he the first among the dead (*Od.* 11.380–387). As Achilles was the runner to be dreaded (*Il.* 20.190, 22.204, cf. 13.324–325, 23.791–792), so now he leaves with long strides (*Od.* 11.539)—long not just because he is a giant, but also because he is sprinting across the asphodel. Odysseus in Troy was described, with the *tl*- root (*Il.* 8.97 and elsewhere), as a daring, enduring man, and such he is said to be still (*Od.* 11.475). There is though one great change: Agamemnon and Achilles now exist in a realm of gloom. When he has drunk of the blood, Agamemnon tells of how Clytemnestra slew him, like an ox at the stall; he then says, as if prophetically, that Odysseus, on his own return, will be luckier far; and finally he asks whether Orestes is alive in Orchomenus, or in Pylos or Sparta. Achilles says he would rather be the poorest serf on earth than rule the nations of the perished, and asks about Neoptolemus— whether he became a warrior and a leader, or not.

A third shade is Ajax, who when he was at Troy "came near, carrying his shield like a tower" (*Il.* 7.219, 11.485, 17.128), and who now is hailed as having been a *tower* among the men in battle. So great is his rancour against Odysseus, though—over the awarding of the arms—that he does not answer him, but joins the other spirits without a word. The afterlife is a blend of being and nonbeing. Agamemnon, Achilles, and Ajax keep a house of impotence and retrospection.

How Dantesque is this Homeric continuum! how Homeric is the Dantesque continuum! Are there two senses—or is there a single sense only—in the resemblance, yet contrast, between the worldly figure and the otherworldly one? To be intelligible but interesting, poets maintain consistency but with change. In the 11th book of the *Odyssey* and in the *Commedia*, the facets of character are seen now under the light of the past, now under that of the present. So we are justified in saying there are two senses, easily distinguished. Or we may say that the literal-anagogical continuum is a single sense only, one of depth, not shallowness. Truly a Byzantine question.

A useful rule is that the shades in Homer, and the souls in Dante, *hold the thought they held at the moment of death*. For Ajax in Homer it is the awarding of the arms to Odysseus; in Dante, it is politics for Farinata, his son Guido for Cavalcante, the code of love for Francesca, the hatefulness of Jove for Capaneus, his *Treasure* for Brunetto, and adventure for Ulysses. Agamemnon in Homer, and Guido da Montefeltro in Dante, hold the thoughts they held a little while *after* death: the one thinks of how Clytemnestra would not close the eyes and mouth of his corpse; the other, of the contention to possess him when he had died. These are special cases; and Ciacco may be another. But by and large the shades and souls have come into the next world just as they left the earthly one. It is a simple rule but it has great strength. Sinclair (on the 4th canto; see also his note on the 26th) says that "Christ is unknown and cannot be named in Hell." No, the souls in hell do not name Christ because they were not thinking of him at the moment of death.

Agamemnon in the *Odyssey* knows of the past, and can tell (as prophecy or guesswork) what awaits Odysseus, but is ignorant of the present—of what has befallen his son. Similarly in the *Inferno*:

> "Like one who has imperfect vision, we see the things," he said, "which are remote from us; so much light the Supreme Ruler still gives to us;
>
> when they draw nigh, or are, our intellect is altogether void; and except what others bring us, we know nothing of your human state.
>
> Therefore thou mayest understand that all our knowledge shall be dead, from that moment when the portal of the Future shall be closed." (*Inf.* 10.100–108, Carlyle trans.)

They know the past but not the present, like those with Alzheimer's disease; but they also know the future. At the last judgment, when time ends, they will be left in a past that has become timeless. Until then, the dead may recognize a pilgrim as a friend, or as a Florentine, and be the readier to converse with him. Sinclair (in a note on the 6th canto) finds it "a curious law, not easily explained" that those in hell should be aware of what has happened, and of what shall happen, but unaware of what is happening. Actually, the law is not hard to explain, as a convention for storytellers, since it furthers talk between the dead and the living. Nor is it curious, since its license lies at hand.

In his essay "On the Care to be Taken for the Dead" (Migne *PL* 40.604–606), Augustine argues—from the early death given as a reward to Josiah (2 Ki. 22) and from the words "though Abraham be ignorant of us" (Isa. 63.15)—that the dead do not know what is happening on earth. They may learn of it, tardily, from those who die later, as Abraham—when he is knowing, not ignorant—must have learned about the lives of the rich man and Lazarus (Lk 16) from Lazarus himself. The dead may also be made aware, by revelation, of things to come. Aquinas, in his monograph *Questions*

About the Soul (article 20 objection 3 and response), refers to this argument, and seems to reason from it. Is Dante indebted to them both? No, the lines "if others do not tell us, we know nothing of your human state" (*Inf.* 10.104–105) sound as if they are owed to Augustine, not to Aquinas, and the same is true for the idea that the dead, though seeing the earthly present dimly, have keen sight for the past and the future (10.100–101).

We have then, for the law that the dead know the past and the future but not the present, two models. The secular one is the *Odyssey*; the sacred one is scripture, with the commentaries of Augustine and Aquinas. Surely Homer is only an analogue, not a source? Yes, but the resemblance is remarkable. Any borrowing from Augustine on the dead can scarcely strike us forcibly. And the Auerbach thesis about figurism weighs lighter than ever. Dante composed in literal and anagogical senses just as his Ionian compeer had done, the *poeta sovrano* himself.

As in the *Odyssey*, so in the *Inferno*, the shades or souls do know something of the present: they know that they are dead and among the dead. With the words of Achilles—that he would rather be the lowliest serf on earth than ruler of the dead—may be compared those of Francesca ("If the king of the universe were a friend," *Inf.* 5.91), Ciacco ("For the damning sin of the gorge," 6.53), Alessio ("Down here the flatteries have sunk me which my tongue was never cloyed with," 18.125–126), and Guido da Montefeltro ("So I am lost where thou seest," 27.128). But in another respect the shades and the souls differ. Agamemnon, Achilles, and Ajax—in not being punished for any wrongdoing—contrast with the memorable figures of the *Inferno*, and resemble only the virtuous heathen (of the 4th canto). So it cannot be an issue in Homer, though it is a crucial one in Dante, whether the dead have repented. Like the shades of the *Odyssey*, the souls of the *Inferno* hold the thought they held at the moment of death, and had they then been repentant they would now be elsewhere, namely in purgatory or paradise. If the souls repent at all (*Inf.* 11.42), it is in their heads, not in their hearts. Each of them has made a confession of sin (5.7–18), but it was without spiritual awareness; I doubt whether we should say that Minos "symbolizes the evil conscience" (Toynbee *Dante dictionary* "Minos"). Guido da Montefeltro is sorry about the bargain he made, for he knows he lost; but there is no compunction in him (27.118). The souls are unrepenting as they were at death; the literal and anagogical senses are continuous truly.

D. The continuum in relation to the moral sense

Those of the lower world, in Dante though not in Homer, are sinful. They died unrepentant; so their last thoughts, which they still hold, may show their sin. But the thoughts may have been upon other matters entirely. The likelihood is that in the *Inferno* there will sometimes, but not always, be a moral bridge to the literal-anagogical continuum. Do we have a strong or a weak impression that the souls are possessed by sin? Brandeis goes too far; Auerbach, not far enough.

Consider whether "the members of Dante's Hell, having died impenitent and come directly into the afterworld, bear their sinfulness with them and are, as we see them, exemplary of it" (Brandeis *Ladder of Vision* p. 24). And whether, "since the soul is all that survives and the sin has characterized the soul, one does better to take *all* that Dante reveals as connected with the sin" than to think him willing to lapse from his subject (same page). No, these formulations are not to be agreed with. The souls do "bear their sinfulness with them," but many also bear earthly concerns clear of sin, and some (like Vanni Fucci blaspheming) embody a different sin than the one they are damned for. That the *Inferno* shows "sin in action" (Brandeis pp. 22–59) has to be abandoned as a partial truth, partial falsehood. Sometimes the moral sense (the topology of sins) is connected to the literal-anagogical continuum (a domain of character); sometimes not.

Alternatively, do we—as the *explication de textes* method requires us to do—both distinguish the work from others, and tell about it a general truth, when we say:

Here in Hell Farinata is greater, stronger, and nobler than ever, for never in his life on earth had he had such an opportunity to prove his stout heart; and if his thoughts and desires centre unchanged upon Florence and the Ghibellines, upon the successes and failures of his former endeavours, there can be no doubt that this persistence of his earthly being in all its grandeur and hopeless futility is part of the judgment God has pronounced upon him. The same hopeless futility in the continuance of his earthly being is displayed by Cavalcante; it is not likely that in the course of his earthly existence he ever felt his faith in the spirit of man, his love for the sweetness of light and for his son so profoundly, or expressed it so arrestingly, as now, when it is all in vain. (Auerbach *Mimesis* p. 193)

No, the elements spoken of are not so singularly Dantesque as the discussion implies, for they are also Homeric. Farinata despises the underworld; so does Achilles. Cavalcante is concerned for his son; so are Agamemnon and Achilles. Both Farinata and Cavalcante think about what happened on earth, not about what is happening now; the same is true for Ajax. So the *explication* has not altogether well distinguished one work from another. The issue remaining is whether for the *Inferno* it has yielded a general truth. Again perhaps not, owing to a special circumstance. Farinata is mindful of politics, and Cavalcante of his son, *because they held there was no afterlife* (10.14–15). They still hold there is none, not taking heed to themselves! They continue to think as at the moment of death, impenitent of their Epicurean heresy. The literal-anagogical continuum has here—but has it elsewhere?—been bridged to the moral sense. Is the episode of Farinata and Cavalcante typical, or is it exceptional?

Mark the souls tossed by a storm in its fury. They are Semiramis and Cleopatra and Helen, and Achilles too (whom love caught at last) and Paris and Tristan; Dido is another; and then there is one more, who speaks:

"Love, which is quickly caught in gentle heart, took him with the fair body of which I was bereft; and the manner still afflicts me.

Love, which to no loved one permits excuse for loving, took me so strongly with delight in him, that, as thou seest, even now it leaves me not.

Love led us to one death; Caïna waits for him who quenched our life." These words from them were offered to us. (Carlyle trans.)

"Amor, che al cor gentil ratto s' apprende,
prese costui della bella persona
che me fu tolta, e il modo ancor m' offende.

Amor, che a nullo amato amar perdona,
mi prese del costui piacer si forte,
che come vedi, ancor non m' abbandona.

Amor condusse noi ad una morte;
Caïna attende chi vita ci spense."
Queste parole da lor ci fur porte. (*Inf.* 5.100–108)

Our comments on Francesca will be worthless if they do not recognize the source of these lines. As Bergin (*Dante* p. 271) mentions, it is the *De arte honeste amandi* of Andreas Capellanus, (here quoted as edited by Locke). Line 100 cor gentil, *gentle* in the sense *noble*; Andreas p. 6 "one woman belongs to the middle class, a second to the simple nobility, and a third to the higher nobility"; love is for those of leisure and caste. Line 101 bella persona; Andreas p. 2 "Love is a certain inborn suffering derived from the sight of and excessive meditation upon the beauty of the opposite sex." Line 103 Amor, che a nullo amato amar perdona; Andreas p. 43 no. 26 "Love can deny nothing to love." Francesca is reciting her creed, the commandments she lived by. She was behaving as her code of manners bade, but it was not wholly learned behaviour, for the code said yes to desire; and these were the last thoughts of her life:

"One day, for pastime, we read of Lancelot, how love constrained him; we were alone, and without all suspicion.

Several times that reading urged our eyes to meet, and changed the colour of our faces; but one moment alone it was that overcame us.

When we read how the fond smile was kissed by such a lover, he, who shall never be divided from me,

kissed my mouth all trembling: the book, and he who wrote it, was a Galeotto; that day we read in it no farther."

"Noi leggevamo un giorno per diletto
di Lancillotto, come amor lo strinse;
soli eravamo e senza alcun sospetto.

Per più fiate gli occhi ci sospinse
quella lettura, e scolorocci il viso;
ma solo un punto fu quel che ci vinse.

Quando leggemmo il disiato riso
esser baciato da cotanto amante,
questi, che mai da me non fia diviso,

la bocca mi baciò tutto tremante:
Galeotto fu il libro, e chi lo scrisse;
quel giorno piu non vi leggemmo avante."

Even here she follows Andreas: "Every lover regularly turns pale in the presence of his beloved" (p. 42 no. 15), and "he strives to get a helper to find an intermediary" (p. 3). Actually, it was the book that blanched their faces, the book that was the pander or Galeotto. To us, the passage in the romance is a philtre none too potent:

"Ah, lady," said Galehot, "doubt not his will thereto, for it is wholly there. And wit ye well that none will see it. Now let us three draw together even as if we were taking counsel together." "Now where-fore should I wait for entreaties?" said the queen. "More do I desire it than either ye or he." Therewithal they all three drew together and made semblance that they took counsel. The queen saw that the knight durst do no more, and she raised his chin, and she kissed him full long in the presence of Galehot, so that the Lady of Malohaut was ware that she kissed him. (*Lancelot* trans. Paton p. 213)

Francesca was fallen before the fall; an Arthurian romance was the last feather. United to her lover (line 105, cf. 74), whom she calls "this man here," she is possessed wholly by courtly love. Nor has she in her heart any awareness of wrongdoing. In the Farinata-Cavalcante episode the literal-anagogical continuum and the moral sense (a warning against heresy) were joined; with Francesca the continuum and the moral sense (a warning against carnal sin) are fused.

As with Francesca so with Capaneus. He assailed Jove with words when he lived, and continues to do so now (14.52–60). It is the locale of the violent against God. Many of them weep from the fire, but he is heedless of it, raging against his Adversary. The literal-anagogical continuum and the moral sense are again as one.

Some of those in a bog are striking each other with hands and feet and teeth; others—beneath the water—can only gurgle what they would say. The two groups are the wrathful and the sullen (*Inf.* 7.109–126). It is a memorable, horrible scene, the crowd shouting "At Filippo Argenti!" Most of the commentators—all of them, I believe—take him as among the wrathful, and think he puts his hands on the boat (8.40) to overturn it. He is really among the sullen, and perhaps—who can say?—would only pull himself from the mire. His words, "Thou seest that I am one who weeps" (line 36), come not from a wrathful man, but from a sullen one. True, they are intelligible, not gurgled into gibberish, but then Virgil had understood the sullen before.

This man was a person of hauteur in the world;
no good is there to ornament his memory;
in the same way here, his shade is furious with himself

Quei fu al mondo persona orgogliosa;
bontà non è che sua memoria fregi:
cosi s' è l'ombra sua qui furiosa. (8.46–48)

(My version of this last line takes account of the reflexive pronoun; Grandgent on 7.94 says a meaningless reflexive was common.)

Filippo Argenti is melancholy, resentful, just as he was when alive; self-devouring, for it is himself, not the others, whom he bites at (line 63). The sin goes on and this is the place for it. The literal-anagogical continuum about him is bridged to the moral sense.

One of the moments no-one forgets is when a twig is plucked from a tree and its trunk cries out: "Why dost thou tear me?" (13.33). It is the grove of suicides, and the injury was done to Pier da Vigne. He had the keys to the heart of the Emperor Frederick (he tells) until the envy of others brought him to disgrace and into taking his life. It is a piteous history, self-destructive. The soul speaks not like a plant, but like a man who is wretched now as before. The moral sense (a warning against suicide) is again bridged to the literal-anagogical continuum.

One of those in a company of baked souls takes Dante by the hem: it is Brunetto. They converse, the younger speaking with the respectful pronoun *voi* (*Inf.* 15.30), the older encouraging him to follow his star (line 55). Who are the others in those environs? They are scholars, men of letters, Priscian for one, all contaminated by the same sin. But now Brunetto must go; asking that his compilation *Treasure* be remembered, he runs like a man who wins a race. Has the episode shown us a sin unrepented of? if so, what sin? sodomy? Brunetto is full of friendly counsels and pride in his volume; sodomy is not a part of him so far as we can see. The literal-anagogical continuum here has nothing to do with the moral sense.

Vanni Fucci tells the story of his crime against the sacristy (24.122–151). Does he regret it, repent of it? The gesture he makes at God (25.3) keeps us from thinking so. The literal and anagogical senses are continuous. Does he in word and deed embody his sin? No, for he was a thief, but he is not thieving now. Similarly with Ulysses, punished as an evil counsellor, for he devised the Trojan Horse. Nothing of this in his narrative, nor in his person, except that he is a tongue, a tongue of flame. Who would distrust him? are there deceits in his words? What everyone hears is a great-hearted desire for new experiences, new adventures:

Consider your origin: ye were not formed to live like brutes, but to follow virtue and knowledge. (Carlyle trans.)

Considerate la vostra semenza:
fatti non foste a viver come bruti,
ma per seguir virtute e conoscenza. (*Inf.* 26.118–120)

For some of the souls in the *Inferno*—Farinata and Cavalcante, Francesca above all, Capaneus, Filippo Argenti, Pier da Vigne—the literal-anagogical continuum is a thoroughfare that merges with the moral sense. For others—Brunetto, Vanni Fucci, Ulysses—the continuum and the moral sense hardly intersect.

E. The punishments within the moral sense

"Even as Paolo is bound through eternity to Francesca by love, so is Ugolino bound eternally by hatred to Ruggiero who betrayed him" (*De Sanctis on Dante* p. 110). Is this summary useful? is it defective? It fails to say that the moral sense is evident in the foreground of the Francesca episode, but hidden in the background of the Ugolino one. She is damned as a carnal sinner and speaks like one. He is damned as a traitor but does not speak like one. What the comment helps us to see is that the souls in hell still think their last thoughts from earth. Francesca was minded towards love. Ugolino was full of hate, and besides he was hungry, and had been led (or almost been led) into cannibalism. What is denoted, what connoted, by the words *più che il dolor potè il digiuno* "fasting had greater power than grief" (*Inf.* 33.75)? One meaning is that death by starvation released him from an agony of sorrow. Another meaning—a likelier one because it furthers the continuum—is that finally he ate the flesh of his children, which "became the flesh of his enemy in

61

his imagination" (*De Sanctis* p. 126). That he betrayed anyone is not what we remember about him. With Francesca there is, with Ugolino there is not, a sameness between the continuum and the moral sense. Both were unrepentant; but she was, he was not, minded upon the damning sin at the moment of death.

Is it not then as punishment that Francesca is united with Paolo, and that Ugolino gnaws at the skull of Ruggieri? We may find the answer by returning into the underworld of the *Odyssey.* Besides Agamemnon, Achilles, and Ajax, who else was there? Minos with a gold sceptre (11.568–569) and Orion herding beasts he had slain in the world above; Tityus with vultures at his liver, Tantalus desiring the water and fruit that recede from him, and Sisyphus pushing a boulder that rolls back down; finally, Heracles, but only his wraith, for he is really among the gods. A greater spectacle, less human interest. How Homeric!—how Dantesque!—is the change from what we were being told of a moment ago.

Surely Tityus, Tantalus, and Sisyphus were behemoths, deserving agonies? Tityus had meant to ravish the goddess Leto (11.578–580); so his being torn at the liver—the seat of the passions—is painful not just to the right degree, but to the right organ as well. There is no looking back to life on earth, though, as there was with Agamemnon, Achilles, and Ajax. The before and after, here, are cause and effect. We could speak of a moral sense, but not of a moral sense aside from—and in addition to—the literal-anagogical continuum. Tantalus, by a myth not mentioned in Homer, had offered a horrible feast to the gods; so *his* suffering too may be condign, ironic. And for him too the continuum of present with past is retribution for wrongdoing. What Sisyphus had done, we cannot well say. Is it all the same in Dante, as with Tityus and Tantalus in Homer; or is it otherwise?

". . . wherewithal a man sinneth, by the same shall he be punished" (Wisdom 11.16, quoted in a headnote to the 33rd canto, Carlyle trans.). The proverb hardly holds for Ciacco the glutton, who lies in a cold rain; but it is touchingly or gloomily or terrifyingly true for many. Because (*Inf.* 28.139) of the unnatural cleavage caused by Bertran de Born, he carries his severed head by the hair; we see in him a counterstep, a contrapasso (line 142). It is

62

poetic justice, as with Tityus and (probably) Tantalus; the repayment is in like coin. And yet between the poems there is a telling twofold difference. First, the Homeric punishments are for individual figures; Tityus bears this torment, Tantalus bears that one. Secondly, except for the punishments, and the crimes being requited, the felons have no existence; Tityus and Tantalus themselves are not of interest. But in the *Inferno* the punishments are each for a class; Bertran de Born suffers much as the other schismatics do, and so for the heretics, or for the hoarders. And, secondly, within a class may be souls whose histories do interest us for their own sakes. Whatever is of the group—such as its punishment—conveys the moral sense. Whatever is exceptional—such as the togetherness of Francesca and Paolo, or of Ugolino and Ruggieri—lies along the literal-anagogical continuum. It is as if their last moments were caught and kept—it is certainly not as punishment—that the two lovers are joined forever, or that the two treacherous are. The moral sense and the continuum (as with Francesca) may be interwoven, but (as with Ugolino) they need not be.

What then do we say of Alberigo, Branca d'Oria, and the others who betrayed their guests? When one commits that sin, the soul falls headlong into the pit, and a devil inhabits the body until the time of death comes (33.118–147). There is authority for this (cited by Sinclair on the passage): Psalms 55 (54) about betrayal by a man who was trusted, with a curse upon such: "let them go down quick into hell." All the same, it is a thrilling surprise. And yet we have seen something comparable. The soul of Alberigo is like the wraith of Heracles, in being below while the body itself is living above. In Dante as in Homer, rules will often yield, and especially will theology yield to poetry. What holds firm is the double principle that the moral sense of the *Inferno* may be taken from the group, and that the literal-anagogical continuum—to a greater or lesser degree—is a chronicle of individuality.

Once Dante had designed—for the moral sense—the arrangement of sins, what questions did he ask himself? The chief ones—independent of each other, neither prior to the other—were no doubt: *What pain should be suffered in this locale?* and *What case histories shall I describe there?* The former of these, being a matter of architecture, would have to do with the moral sense; the latter would have to do with the literal-anagogical continuum. The result is, the answers to the former question are great, but those to the latter are greater. "The tremendous pattern was broken by the overwhelming power of the images it had to contain" (Auerbach *Mimesis* p. 202). The diagrams that may accompany our texts are not a précis of the poem; a better précis would be a selection of the words spoken by Francesca, Farinata, Brunetto, Ulysses, Ugolino, and the others.

F. The fourth sense and the fourfold scheme

Though reluctant to find four strata of meaning throughout the *Commedia*, Grayson (in *The World of Dante* pp. 160–161) does allow that "the procession in the Earthly Paradise," from the *Purgatorio*, is an episode "with obvious allegorical significance." At its climax the appearance of Beatrice "is a figure of the appearance of Christ" (Auerbach in *Speculum* 21:481; cf. Singleton in *Romanic Review* 42:177, "Beatrice comes—as Christ"). It is allegory not just in the generic, but in the specific sense, = typology; at least, it *may* be. The great specimen of the fourth sense lies elsewhere, though—at the climax not of the *Purgatorio*, but of the *Inferno*.

The lowest circle of hell holds—in regions named after Cain, Antenor, Ptolemy, and Judas—those who betrayed kinsman, state, guest, and benefactor. (Sinclair on the 33rd canto notes that the betrayed may be regarded as exemplars: Abel, humanity; the Trojans, the Romans; the high priest Maccabeus, the Church; and Christ, God.) With Judas in the deepest region are Brutus and Cassius; the three are being crunched in the jaws of a triple-headed Lucifer: that is the literal sense. Why does Brutus, writhing, not utter a sound? Because he had, and has, the fortitude to withstand anguish; he is not insensible (see *Paradiso* 6.74), but his howlings are muted by the Stoicism he was reared in. The literal and anagogical senses are continuous. What did Brutus and Cassius have in common with Judas? The assassins had been pardoned by Caesar; the false disciple had been given healing by Jesus (Mt 10.1, Mk 3.15). So they are in the place of those who betrayed their benefactor: that is the moral sense.

The fourth, allegorical (typological) sense is the remarkable one, though, and we have not seen it in the poem elsewhere. Christ and Caesar are like antitype and type; it is as if Christ had been prefigured by Caesar, and Judas by Brutus and Cassius. The poet has made two events—the betrayal of Christ and the betrayal of Caesar—congrue as a mystery in the scheme of things.

Is Lucifer being punished in Giudecca, the locale of Judas? Sinclair (on the 34th canto) holds that Lucifer here is thought of "not so much as a personal sinner, but rather as the last and greatest of Hell's monsters." There is some truth in this, for he is a torture machine. Opposite to God absolutely, he is not just in, he *is*, the place of those that were false to the ones who had done them goodness. But yes he too is suffering punishment. In *Paradise Lost* (2.689) Satan is called a traitor, and in the *Inferno* Lucifer has his seat where every traitor is eternally punished (11.64), for he lifted up his brows against his maker (34.35). The literal-anagogical continuum is in magnitude, the change being from positive to negative: Lucifer is now the most hideous of created things as once he was the most beautiful. The moral sense is that betrayal of a benefactor—disloyalty with ingratitude—is the sin more terrible than any other. The allegorical (typological) sense is that the betrayal of God prefigured those of Christ and of Caesar. We could say that the world twice reenacted the primal sin.

I find then in the canto a combining of four stupendous conceptions, two of them having to do with the allegorical (typological) sense, two with the moral. First, that Lucifer and Judas might be type and antitype; the devil does enter into Judas in the gospels (Lk. 22.3, Jn 13.2), but that idea is a simpler one. Second, that Brutus and Cassius might be types or foreshadowings of Judas; typology had so far studied only the resemblances between the Old Testament and the New, not those between secular history and sacred. Third, that the same crime was committed against the most high in sacred history as in secular: God, Christ, and Caesar. Fourth, that this very crime should *for theoretical, nonhistorical reasons alone* be regarded as the most vile; it is the greatest of sins *even without a view to who the victims are.* Lucifer, Judas, Brutus and Cassius are at the centre of hell from considerations in typology and also from wholly distinct considerations in ethics.

The sins of incontinence are less grave; those of force, more grave; and those of fraud, the gravest: so tells the 11th canto of the *Inferno.* This was after Aristotle (*Nicomachean Ethics* 7.1.1.,7.6.7), Cicero (*De officiis* 1.13), and Aquinas (*Summa Theologica* first part of the 2nd part, question 73, article 5): see Moore (*Studies in Dante* 2nd ser. p. 157). What Dante added was the subdividing, as of fraud into deception and betrayal, and the further subdividing as of betrayal into crimes against kinsman, state, guest, and benefactor. The poet has *justified on philosophical grounds alone* (without respect to persons!) the putting of Judas, and Lucifer, into the bowels of hell.

The custom among authors is to conceive of the climax and then of the middle and the beginning. So I would suggest that Dante thought to himself as follows. (1) Lucifer (as the adversary of God) is to be at the centre of hell, and so is Judas (for his wrong against Christ). (2) They cannot be paired as equals, but a gigantic Lucifer—himself in agony—can be the instrument of agony for Judas. (3) What they have in common, other than in having sinned against the Father and the Son, is hard to see: let the rebellion of Lucifer be offered, though not forcibly, as a grand-scale betrayal. (4) With Judas let others of the same fault be punished, if there are any whose victim is comparable to Christ; Brutus and Cassius come to mind, for Caesar ruled temporal Rome as Christ (through the papacy) rules spiritual Rome, the see of both empire and church. (5) The crime of Judas, and of Brutus and Cassius, and of Lucifer as well, should be taken as somehow *in itself* the worst one that can be committed. (6) Let it be taken as a kind of fraud, which according to Aristotle is ten thousand times more harmful than brutishness, mere incontinence being yet less grave: all the sins can afterwards be arranged under these three headings. (7) The particular form of betrayal that Judas and the others—even Lucifer—have in common is the betrayal of a benefactor; near to it let the other forms of betrayal be punished; and let the other forms of fraud than betrayal be punished less deep than in the bowels.

Now for the number of higher senses. The allegorical (typological) sense: this is the uncanny one, of the utmost power in the 34th canto, but perhaps nowhere else in the *Commedia*. The moral sense: largely consisting in the abodes after death of those who were unrepentant *(Inferno)* or repentant *(Purgatorio)* of various sins, or were marked by various virtues *(Paradiso)*; a pervasive background. The anagogical sense: how it resembles the literal sense! how continuous—for Francesca, Ugolino, Brunetto, Ulysses, Capaneus—the otherworldly with the worldly sense! In the 34th canto, which I regard as the cornerstone of the hundred, all three of the higher senses can be counted. But the allegorical (typological) sense—and its conformity with the moral sense—are the matters to wonder at. Elsewhere, if the literal-anagogical continuum is taken to be a single sense only, there is but one higher sense—the moral—and it is praiseworthy but no more than that.

III. When in *Othello* is the marriage, when the consummation?

A text from Deuteronomy 22 is most relevant:

> If a man take a wife and when he hath lain with her hate her and lay shameful things unto her charge and bring up an evil name upon her and say: I took this wife, and when I came to her, I found her not a maid: Then let the father of the damsel and the mother bring forth the tokens of the damsel's virginity, unto the elders of the city (Tyndale's version)

Blood is shed at the loss of virginity. That is (almost) a fact of life. Mary McCarthy writes about it in *The Group*. Shakespeare, in *Othello*, does not, not directly; he alludes to it, and we are aware of it; but then matters take another turn.

The chief, though not the first scholar to speak about the evidence of virginity in *Othello* is Boose, in *English Literary Renaissance* 5 (1975). She regards the handkerchief as "a visually recognizable reduction of Othello and Desdemona's wedding-bed sheets, the visual proof of their consummated marriage" (p. 363), and takes the strawberries embroidered on the handkerchief to be "emblematic of virgin blood" (p. 362). It is not Freudian psychology, but "evidence on the implicit level of the connections in Shakespeare's own mind between token and sexual consummation and those he could expect his audience to perceive between strawberry-spotted handkerchief and blood-spotted sheets" (p. 366). The savagery of the close is then tragic irony: "not only does Othello murder Desdemona over her inability to produce the very handkerchief he had himself seen in her hand just a short time previously, but he also executes as a whore the very bride whose virginal fidelity he physically experienced but hours earlier" (p. 368).

There is a special reason why the evidence of virginity should have been important in a play about a Moor, dating from 1604. An account of Morocco was published in 1600, in London: Pory's translation of *A Geographical History of Africa* by Leo Africanus. Did Shakespeare know of it? If not directly, then (I assume) indirectly. The third book tells of the wedding custom in Araby:

> a certain woman standeth before the bride-chamber door, expecting till the bridegroom having deflowered his bride reacheth her a napkin stained with blood, which napkin she carrieth incontinent and showeth to the guests, proclaiming with a loud voice that the bride was ever till that time an unspotted and pure virgin.

Cinthio, the source for *Othello*, has nothing of this. It was to be added: a theatrical element, a knot tying together the strands of chastity, barbarism, blood, and visual proof.

The association of such evidence with the handkerchief is by no means fanciful. Leo Africanus, as rendered by Pory, used the word *napkin*, rather than *sheet* or *cloth*; and the handkerchief is repeatedly called a napkin in the play (3.3.287, 290, 321). Besides, Burckhardt *Arabic Proverbs* (2nd ed. p. 140) remarks that

> Among the lower classes of Moslems at Cairo it is customary that on the day after the nuptials certain female relations of the bride should carry her innermost garment (not her handkerchief as some travellers have related) in triumph to the houses of their neighbours.

". . . not her *handkerchief*." Perhaps the coincidence is meaningless; but perhaps the handkerchief of the play is from travellers' talk at the Mermaid tavern. So a latent suggestion of what Deuteronomy calls *tokens* is not only probable in *napkin*, but even possible in *handkerchief*. Moreover, Desdemona speaks of the handkerchief as being a *token* (5.2.61), and so does Othello (5.2.217).

Where I differ absolutely from Boose and other commentators is on the consummation of the marriage. Did it really occur during the first night on Cyprus? Are the wedding sheets (4.2.104, 4.3.24) really displayed as tokens of Desdemona's virginity? Would they not unsay that Cassio had been her lover? Can the Moor be less aware than we are of a Moorish proof? If there is an inconsistency here, it is the starkest one in Shakespeare.

Act 1 (scenes 1–3), at Venice.

. . . an old black ram Is tupping your white ewe (1.1.88–89) . . . you'll have your daughter covered with a Barbary horse; you'll have your nephews neigh to you (1.1.111–112) . . . your daughter and the Moor are now making the beast with two backs (1.1.114–115) . . . Are they married, think you? (1.1.166) . . . Are you fast married? (1.2.11) . . . true I have married her (1.3.79) . . . But here's my husband (1.3.185) . . . if I be left behind, A moth of peace, and he go to the war, The rites for which I love him are bereft me (1.3.256–257) . . . the young affects In me defunct (1.3.263–264)

It must be true that Othello and Desdemona have just eloped, just been married. What was the ceremony like? It would be hard to say. Have they come together sexually since the wedding? Evidently not: Desdemona's words "The rites for which I love him are bereft me" argue either way; but Othello's words "the young affects In me defunct" are scarcely the speech of a bridegroom who has for the first time known his bride. But may not Othello and Desdemona have come together before marriage? It would not sort well with either the nobility of Othello or the honor of Desdemona. Did she before marriage have Cassio or someone else as a lover? Unbelievable. So she is a virgin: we think it in the rear of our mind; but we do not affirm it, for her chastity has not become an issue. What we sense is that this is the wedding night of Othello and Desdemona. Brabantio would appeal to the Duke against the Moor's beguiling of his daughter. But now a message comes of the Turkish fleet at Cyprus; so the Duke would summon Othello for this second cause. Not only has Brabantio's sleep been interrupted, but also the consummation of the marriage: so we gather without being told outright. The whole act takes place in a very short time—no longer than the time of the players on stage—and is of course a masterpiece.

Between Acts 1 and 2, an interval, with change of scene to Cyprus
for the rest of the play.

How much time elapsed in the sailing from Venice to Cyprus?
Why, no time at all. In the *Agamemnon* of Aeschylus the beacon
flashes, signalling that Troy has fallen; and in a moment the great
king arrives home: "the sooner the better," says Page in his
commentary (p. xxxiii): the dramatic time is nil. In the *Eumenides* we
see Orestes now before the temple of Apollo at Delphi, now before
the temple of Athene at Athens; but the change in both place and
time is negligible, for the scene looks the same and the action is
continuous. Likewise with the change in place and time, but continuity of action, in *Othello*. ". . . the bold Iago, Whose footing
here anticipates our thoughts A se'nnight's speed," says Cassio
(2.1.76–77), which means in a practical sense that the trip, for
Iago, is over a week earlier than one would have thought; matters
go on without a halt. What then of the marriage between Othello
and Desdemona? Its consummation has been postponed a sailing-
time, but we are not conscious of the wait, and we do not know
that they are conscious of it.

Act 2 (scenes 1–3).

He hath achieved a maid That paragons description and wild fame
(2.1.61–62) . . . That he may bless this bay with his tall ship, Make
love's quick pants in Desdemona's arms (2.1.79–80) . . . When the
blood is made dull with the act of sport, there should be, again to
inflame it and to give satiety a fresh appetite, loveliness in favor,
sympathy in years, manners, and beauties; all which the Moor is
defective in (2.1.224–228) . . . I do suspect the lusty Moor Hath
leaped into my seat (2.1.289–290) . . . it is the celebration of his
nuptial (2.2.7) . . . from the present hour of five till the bell have told
eleven (2.2.9) . . . Come, my dear love. The purchase made, the
fruits are to ensue; That profit's yet to come 'tween me and you
(2.3.9–11) . . . 'tis not yet ten o' th' clock (2.3.13) . . . He hath not yet
made wanton the night with her (2.3.16) . . . happiness to their

sheets (2.3.26) . . . Friends all, but now, even now, In quarter, and in terms like bride and groom Devesting them for bed; and then, but now—As if some planet had unwitted men—Swords out, and tilting at other's breast In opposition bloody (2.3.169–174) . . . Cassio, I love thee; But never more be officer of mine. Look if my gentle love be not raised up! (2.3.239–241) . . . All's well now, sweeting; come away to bed (2.3.243) . . . This broken joint between you and her husband entreat her to splinter (2.3.308) . . . By the mass, 'tis morning! (2.3.360)

Cassio's tribute to Desdemona (2.1.61–62) confirms our impression of her. That the marriage was consummated before the scene shifted to Cyprus seems more impossible than ever. The postponed wedding night, the night of their first sexual union, is to be now, coinciding with the festivity for the wreck of the Turkish fleet; and Iago thinks of the marriage sheets (2.3.26) and of bride and groom (2.3.170). But the night is broken open by the drunken quarrel. Othello degrades Cassio, and Desdemona is roused, too. The pair return to bed; but it is almost morning. When did they come together, before the interruption or after? or at both times, or at neither time? We cannot say when, which means that we cannot say whether. But the tranquillity of the night, entrusted to Cassio, was ruined by his weakness. The dramatic impression is that the hours both before and after the hubbub fleeted away in a moment; the breach of the peace was the chief and central happening between twilight and dawn. We may have the impression, though vaguely (since no words tell of it), that Iago caused Othello to be summoned just when he was about to know his bride for the first time.

Act 3 (scenes 1–4).

Masters, play here, I will content your pains (3.1.1) . . . the day had broke Before we parted (3.1.31) . . . My lord shall never rest; I'll watch him tame and talk him out of patience; His bed shall seem a school, his board a shrift; I'll intermingle everything he does With Cassio's suit (3.3.22–26) . . . Was not that Cassio parted from my wife? (3.3.37) . . . Why then, to-morrow night, or Tuesday morn, Or

Tuesday noon or night, or Wednesday morn (3.3.60) . . . Farewell, my Desdemon: I'll come to thee straight (3.3.87) . . . And when I told thee he was of my counsel In my whole course of wooing, thou cried'st "Indeed?" (3.3.111) . . . what damnèd minutes tells he o'er Who dotes, yet doubts (3.3.169) . . . That we can call these delicate creatures ours, And not their appetites! (3.3.269) . . . Your napkin is too little; Let it alone (3.3.287) . . . My wayward husband hath a hundred times Wooed me to steal it (3.3.292) . . . What sense had I of her stol'n hours of lust? I saw't not, thought it not, it harmed not me; I slept the next night well (3.3.338–340) . . . I had been happy if the general camp, Pioners and all, had tasted her sweet body, So I had nothing known (3.3.345–347) . . . give me the ocular proof (3.3.360) . . . I think my wife be honest, and think she is not (3.3.384) . . . then laid his leg Over my thigh, and sighed, and kissed, and then Cried "Cursèd fate that gave thee to the Moor!" (3.3.424) . . . Have you not sometimes seen a handkerchief Spotted with strawberries (3.3.434) . . . This hand is moist, my lady (3.4.36) . . . That handkerchief Did an Egyptian to my mother give (3.4.56) . . . It is not lost. But what an if it were? (3.4.84) . . . I am most unhappy in the loss of it (3.4.102) . . . 'Tis not a year or two shows us a man. They are all but stomachs, and we all but food; They eat us hungerly, and when they are full They belch us (3.4.103–106) . . . Nay, we must think men are not gods, Nor of them look for such observancy As fits the bridal (3.4.148–150) . . . And I was going to your lodging, Cassio. What, keep a week away? (3.4.172)

The act begins with music for the bridal pair; we might have thought it would be acknowledged with mention of the sexual union; but things turn out differently. From Desdemona's taking up of Cassio's suit (3.3.22–26) we gather nothing. But from Othello's words "That we can call these delicate creatures ours, And not their appetites" (3.3.269) we gather something, namely that he has not just a short while ago lain with her. He speaks of "her stol'n hours of lust" with Cassio (3.3.338), which he would not have done if she had just proved a virgin. The phrase "I slept the next night well" (3.3.340) refers to heaven knows when, and is not inconsistent with anything. "This hand is moist, my lady" (3.4.36): if Othello reproves Desdemona for signs of lubricity, it may be because she has been chaste towards him. It is not "such observancy as fits the bridal," and perhaps for a reason: the marriage has not been completed, not consummated. The decorum is such that we are not sure what has happened between them.

Act 4 (scenes 1–3).

Or to be naked with her friend in bed An hour or more, not meaning any harm? (4.1.3–4) . . . She is protectress of her honour too; May she give that? (4.1.15) . . . Nature would not invest herself in such shadowing passion without some instruction (4.1.39) . . . This is his second fit; he had one yesterday (4.1.51) . . . For I will make him tell the tale anew—Where, how, how oft, how long ago, and when He hath, and is again to cope your wife (4.1.84–86) . . . If that the earth could teem with woman's tears, Each drop she falls would prove a crocodile (4.1.238–239) . . . For if she be not honest, chaste, and true, There's no man happy (4.2.17) . . . Was this fair paper, this most goodly book, Made to write "whore" upon? (4.2.71) . . . If to preserve this vessel for my lord From any other foul unlawful touch Be not to be a strumpet, I am none (4.2.84–86) . . . Prithee to-night Lay on my bed my wedding sheets (4.2.104) . . . The jewels you have had from me to deliver to Desdemona would half have corrupted a votarist (4.2.188) . . . Get you to bed on th' instant (4.3.7) . . . Give me my nightly wearing, and adieu (4.3.15) . . . I have laid those sheets you bade me on the bed (4.3.21) . . . If I do die before thee, prithee shroud me In one of those same sheets (4.3.23)

The Act has to do with "Where, how, how oft, how long ago, and when" (4.1.85) Desdemona has lain with Cassio. You and I know that the answer to *When?* is never. She is—with cause—a liar: such she has already proved herself to be (is the handkerchief lost?), and such she will prove herself again (who has smothered her?); but she surely does not lie in claiming to preserve a vessel for her lord (4.2.84). Will not Othello and Desdemona come together presently? That is the other subject of the Act. We expect or at least hope that they will. And we have been led to foresee that the wedding sheets will somehow testify to her honour. There is no sketching of definite pictures beforehand, though. Nor has evil been averted. The Moor and his Venetian bride are still unschooled in each other.

Act 5 (scenes 1–2).

Thy bed, lust-stained, shall with lust's blood be spotted (5.1.36) . . . Yet I'll not shed her blood, Nor scar that whiter skin of hers than snow, And smooth as monumental alabaster. Yet she must die (5.2.3–6) . . . Will you come to bed, my lord (5.2.24) . . . never loved Cassio But with such general warranty of heaven As I might love. I never gave him token (5.2.59–61) . . . It was a handkerchief, an antique token My father gave my mother (5.2.217–218) . . . Cold, cold, my girl? Even like thy chastity (5.2.276–277)

In the first line quoted here, how is the bed lust-stained? Has it been marred with semen, or with blood? If with semen, is it Cassio's only, or Othello's as well? If with blood (shed during what the sonnet calls lust in action), how will that contrast with lust's blood? I find the only answer to be that, except for Othello's imaginings, the bed is not stained at all. If he has already shed Desdemona's blood in taking her virginity, will not his words about not shedding her blood sound imperfect? If he had done so, the words would do so; it is all contrary to fact. We looked for the wedding sheets to be displayed and spoken of; we thought they would be, or might be, the tokens of Deuteronomy. It was a hope in vain, perhaps the unhappier when Desdemona (5.2.61) and then Othello (5.2.217) call the handkerchief a token. What of the lines "Cold, cold, my girl? Even like thy chastity"? Do they mean "like thy faithfulness in marriage" or "like thy virginity"? The play ends, and there is no telling; but virginity is the better answer.

How much time has elapsed in the play? There was a night in Venice (Act 1); an interval for sailing; an afternoon, evening, and night on Cyprus (Act 2); the following day and its evening, still on Cyprus (Acts 3–5). But is not this "short time" of the foreground at odds with a "long time" in the background? Are there not indications of a wholly different timeframe? The most arresting one is the first dialogue between Cassio and Bianca:

B. Save you, friend Cassio!
C.   What make you from home?
   How is't with you, my most fair Bianca?
   I' faith, sweet love, I was coming to your house.
B. And I was going to your lodging, Cassio.
   What, keep a week away? seven days and nights?
   Eightscore eight hours? and lovers' absent hours,
   More tedious than the dial eightscore times?
   O weary reck'ning!
C.   Pardon me, Bianca:
   I have this while with leaden thoughts been pressed;
   But I shall in a more continuate time
   Strike off this score of absence. Sweet Bianca,
   Take me this work out.
B.   O Cassio, whence came this?
   This is some token from a newer friend.
   To the felt absence now I feel a cause. (3.4.169–182)

It has not been said who Bianca is. She seems to be a Cypriot, for she has a permanent residence, a home or house, whereas Cassio has only a lodging. Did he become acquainted with her, has he made love to her, on Cyprus? It may be that she lives in a bawdy-house, and has sailed to the island as a camp follower. Venice controlled Cyprus from 1489 to 1571, and if the action of the play is within that period, we might expect to see a Venetian courtesan, a sailors' companion, who travels from bordello to bordello, from city to colony. Cassio may then have known Bianca at Venice, and not on Cyprus only. We listen in on what the two of them say to each other, but the dramatist is not explaining things to us. There is puzzlement, but no real "long time." The double perspective does not rest with time, it rests with marriage.

When is the marriage completed? when do the two come together? Not the first night, for it is interrupted; the second night is the one proclaimed.

In the Second Act, Othello and his Bride go the first time to Bed (Rymer in the Dean *Casebook* p. 118)

(Othello) takes Desdemona from her father's house and marries her, and does not consummate the marriage till they arrive in Cyprus (Daniel "Time-Analysis" p. 229)

the very morrow of the reunion and of the consummation of the marriage (Granville-Barker *Prefaces* p. 143)

only one day separates Desdemona's union with Othello and her murder (Herford in the *Arden* ed. p. 165)

that at the end of Act II they are consummating their marriage and that from the beginning of Act III on they have been long married (Allen in *Shakespeare Survey* 21:20)

This second night, though, is interrupted too. Cassio who was to guard the peace caused the alarum to break into the wedding chamber. Had not the night already served its purpose? If it had not, was the rest of the night useless? The fracas gives the impression of having ruined the ceremony. The interruption of the second night, in Act 2, is like that of the first, in Act 1. The tokens from the Moorish, Levantine custom would have changed our impression; but they are not displayed, not now. The handkerchief is seen instead, and it is called a napkin; it is a simple cloth, such as one might bind an ache with; only later is it a magical heirloom and a pledge of love. It may be a symbol to Othello of the marriage tokens, creative and tortured as he is; it can scarcely be such a symbol to us.

Surely the wedding sheets, which Desdemona speaks of and then Emilia, will be the tokens of virginity, the "ocular proof" not of guilt but of innocence. They will be so in one of those scenes that do not occur. Surely the Trojans when they strip the arms from Achilles will say in astonishment, *It's Patroclus!* Surely when Odysseus, filthy with the blood of the suitors, is bathed and anointed, and then clothed in a fair robe, or *pharos*, he will be told that Penelope, in a ruse of delay, wove it as a shroud for Laertes. No, we expected those scenes, vaguely, but they do not actually exist. We may say that Shakespeare, in preparing us for a high moment but then withholding it because the surprise would no longer be great enough, shares a device with Homer.

A better analogy is with the *Libation Bearers*. One of the momentous questions unasked is "Who suckled Orestes?" Clytemnestra would seem to have done so. She dreamed that she gave birth to a serpent, wrapped it in swaddling clothes, and offered it her breast, from which it sucked milk and gore. The dream may be a presentiment, and Orestes, hearing of it, interprets the serpent as himself. Moreover, Clytemnestra bares her breast to him, and pleads that he think of the time she nursed him, and not kill her. The appeal is an *artistic* one, though, a quotation from Hecuba, as anyone in the 5th-century B.C. audience would have recognized. And, besides, a slave woman has already reminisced of when she cared for Orestes as a baby: she seems to have been what Eurycleia was to Odysseus, which is, a wet-nurse. But then Orestes does kill Clytemnestra, and does in doing so somehow fulfil the dream. Who then had suckled him in infancy? Really, by the end of the play we cannot tell.

It is clear in the *Iliad* that the Trojans will recognize Patroclus. It is unclear in the *Odyssey* whether the *pharos* woven to be a shroud becomes the very one that Odysseus is enrobed in; but little depends on the answer, no more than elegance of motif. It is unclear in the *Oresteia* who suckled Orestes, and much depends on the answer: for the closer the bond was between him and Clytemnestra, the greater the right of the furies to possess him. In *Othello* we do not finally learn whether the wedding sheets are blood-stained with the virginity of Desdemona, or not; and here, too, much depends on the answer. But we *almost* know: for everything said and done is believable if and only if the two of them have not come together.

If the sheets are bloodstained, either because they have not been laundered or because the stain has resisted laundering, we would ask: (1) Have they been laid on the bed (4.2.104, 4.3.21), where one would lie on them? An unseemly idea, a contamination, an abhorrence. (2) Might a corpse be wrapped in them (4.3.23)? Again, unseemly, abhorrent. (3) How can Othello fail to see them, displayed however they may be? and if they were stained only the previous night, how can he think Desdemona a whore? On the other hand, if a bloodstain has been removed by laundering, how do the sheets differ from other laundered ones? The answer must be neither here nor there. The marriage has not been consummated. The wedding sheets are unused, virginal. There is a thought that they will be bloodstained in the future—a proof of innocence. That is all we can say; but I believe we are pretty sure of it, without consciously thinking about it.

If the marriage was not consummated, why not? Is Othello impotent or Desdemona frigid? Egregious ideas. He does say that the young affects are in him defunct (1.3.264) and that he is declined into the vale of years (3.3.266), and Iago—though saying for the sake of slander that Othello is lusty—remarks that the Moor does not have the advantage of youth (2.1.228). But Othello's words "O curse of marriage, that we can call these delicate creatures ours, and not their appetites" make sexual failure on his part out of the question. But do not those words speak against Desdemona? That is impossible too: her words "the rites for which I love him" (1.3.256) mean that she is or will be his wife fully, not by contract only. But passion between them, such as Rosalind speaks of—"they will together: clubs cannot part them" (*As You Like It* 5.2.41)—we do not find. Their love is fragile, delicate; there is still a strangeness in their affection. She has been chaste not only with regard to other men, but with regard to him also. So we might gather, unconsciously, from their circumspect demeanour, and from his last words to her, "Cold, cold, my girl, even like thy chastity." And from the nonappearance of the tokens, as from the line "Yet I'll not shed her blood," we would gather that he has not, in any way, shed her blood yet. But the matter is unspoken of; there is an aspect of mystery; nor do we reflect upon it in the theatre.

Othello (as I understand him) is an unsatisfied lover; more important, he is a disappointed lover, who thought he had won. More important yet, he is an unmarried husband, a defrauded lover: "the purchase made, the fruits are to ensue" (2.3.10). Is it nonnaturalistic that he should be susceptible to jealousy? No, any of us would be. The blame for the brawl on Cyprus, which

interrupted his (postponed) wedding night, falls partly on him, for
he might have planned better; but mostly the blame falls on Cassio
(and Iago). This too is crippling; for Cassio had not been an enemy,
whom trouble was likely from; he had been a friend close to the
heart: it was a violation of trust. What then if Othello senses (or is
led to sense) that Cassio, seeing him coming, steals away guilty-
like? Why, he will think false things of him. Betrayed once,
betrayed again. Same man, same woman. To curse and strike
Desdemona, to fall into a fit, is not this wholly naturalistic?

Sometimes in Shakespeare (a philosopher could say) the poetry
is not really suitable to either the character or the situation. The
gorgeous language of Othello, though, befits him as well as could
be, for he is a raconteur. Are they not fables, even improvisations,
those stories of his? Was it an Egyptian charmer (3.4.56), or was it
his father (5.2.218), who gave the handkerchief to his mother? No,
the tales are not lies; that is not the right word for them; they are of
another world as Othello is. I believe too that his speech, as gaudy
as English will allow, has been made fluent by longing and pain:

> The worms were hallowed that did breed the silk;
> And it was dyed in mummy which the skillful
> Conserved of maidens' hearts (3.4.73–75)
> . . .
>   Yet I'll not shed her blood,
> Nor scar that whiter skin of hers than snow,
> And smooth as monumental alabaster.
> Yet she must die (5.2.3–6)
> . . .
>   Then must you speak
> Of one that loved not wisely, but too well;
> Of one not easily jealous, but, being wrought,
> Perplexed in the extreme; of one whose hand,
> Like the base Judean, threw a pearl away
> Richer than all his tribe; of one whose subdued eyes,
> Albeit unusèd to the melting mood,
> Drop tears as fast as the Arabian trees
> Their med'cinable gum. Set you down this.
> And say besides that in Aleppo once,

Marriage in Othello

Where a malignant and a turbaned Turk
Beat a Venetian and traduced the state,
I took by th' throat the circumcisèd dog
And smote him—thus (5.2.343–356)

We began with a verse, about the tokens of virginity, from Deuteronomy 22. A second verse from that same chapter is also most relevant: "Thou shalt not plow with an ox and an ass together." There is a horror of miscegenation in these words, and there is such a horror in the play: "an old black ram is tupping your white ewe" (1.1.88–89). Many of us in the United States, being ourselves racially mixed, cannot believe that a union of black and white violates nature. But the Othello and Desdemona of Shakespeare, as a pair, are naught if they are not shocking. What will the children be like? It would be an untoward, annoying question, and we ought to be the farther from asking it because of our deep, unspoken realization that Othello and Desdemona have not, in fact, ever come together.

A third verse from Deuteronomy 22 is relevant no less: "The woman shall not wear that which pertaineth unto the man, neither shall a man put on woman's raiment." We are reminded that Desdemona was a boy, and that such female impersonation, perhaps more than any other consideration, led the Puritans to close the theatres in 1642. Morality aside, how did the dramatist make it credible that a male disguised should be his heroine? The plot was a good one, given the convention. For the strangeness, the exotic beauty of Othello, would distract us from noticing the sameness in sex, between the actors. And, besides, the indications—and general likelihood—that the marriage has never taken place, in bed, quiet our sense that Desdemona is not really a woman.

IV. When in *Beowulf* is beer drunk, or mead, when ale or wine?

Dorothy Galton, a correspondent "interested in both beekeeping and history," wrote to the *Times Literary Supplement* on 19 March 1971, about *Beowulf*. Believing "that in the poem the Geats drank mead, while others drank beer," she inferred that they were "a honey-gathering people," and identified them as the Gety, a tribe living on land that is now northern Czechoslovakia and southern Poland. The letter provoked some response, and the whole matter was reported in the *Old English Newsletter* for December 1973. It ought to have been added that the argument was futile since the basic observation was incorrect. The Geats do drink mead (Hygd fills their mead-cups, line 1980), but they do not drink *only* mead (Wiglaf speaks of their beer-hall, 2635); nor do the other nations drink only beer (the Danes empty many a mead-cup, 1015).

Perhaps there is some other rule, having to do not with nationality, but with the season, or with sex or age, or degree of valour. On 7 April 1779, Dr Johnson "shook his head, and said, 'Poor stuff! No, Sir, claret is the liquor for boys; port, for men; but he who aspires to be a hero (smiling) must drink brandy'" (from Boswell's *Life*). Or can it be that one kind of person uses one word, another another? The Old Norse poem *Alvíssmal* (34) tells that while men speak of *ale* and the gods of *beer*, the giants say *pure draught*, and those in hell, *mead*. These are the four main terms in Old English, except that *pure draught* is replaced by *wine*. Does any law govern their use? The *Beowulf* passages to be scanned number about forty.

after beer-taking	had dwelt in	
æfter beoþege	gebun hæfdon	117
very often boasted	drunk with beer	
ful oft gebeotedon	beore druncne	480

82

that they in beer-hall   would abide
þæt hie in beorsele   bidan woldon   482

in beer-hall   a bench cleared
on beorsele   benc gerymed   492

drunk with beer   about Breca spakest
beore druncen   ymb Brecan spræce   531

bade him be blithe   at the beer-taking
bæd hine bliðne   æt þære beorþege   617

in beer-hall   would encourage
on beorsele   byldan wolde   1094

with beds and bolsters;   one of the beer-warriors
beddum ond bolstrum;   beorscealca sum   1240

then says at beer   he who the bague sees
þonne cwið æt beore   se þe beah gesyhð   2041

in beer-hall   he who gave us the bagues
in biorsele   ðe us ðas beagas geaf   2635

over ale-flagon   war-knights
ofer ealowæge   oretmecgas   481

he who in his hands bore   crafted ale-flagon
se þe on handa bær   hroden ealowæge   495

for earls an ale-fest;   angry were both
eorlum ealuscerwen;   yrre wæron begen   769

on ale-bench   to another give
in ealobence   oðrum gesellan   1029

ale-drinkers   said otherwise
ealodrincende   oðer sædan   1945

when he on ale-bench   often gave
þonne he on ealubence   oft gesealde   2867

control of the wine-lodge   and this word said
winærnes geweald,   ond þæt word acwæð   654

in the wine-hall   savage death seized
in þæm winsele   wældeað fornam   695

waded under welkin   till he the wine-building
wod under wolcnum   to þæs þe he winreced   714

then was great wonder   that the wine-hall
þa wæs wundor micel   þæt se winsele   771

wights and women,   who the wine-building
wera ond wifa,   þe þæt winreced   993

wine from wonder-vats;   then came Wealhtheo forth
win of wunderfatum;   þa cwom Wealhþeo forð   1162

wights drank wine;   wyrd they knew not
druncon win weras;   wyrd ne cuðon   1233

drunk with wine,   when he the weapon lent
wine druncen,   þa he þæs wæpnes onlah   1467

wine-hall deserted,   windy resting-place
winsele westne,   windge reste   2456

from many tribes   mead-settles took away
monegum mægþum   meodosetla ofteah   5

a great mead-lodge   men to build
medoærn micel   men gewyrcean   69

then was this mead-hall   at morningtide
ðonne wæs þeos medoheal   on morgentid   484

to mead in mood   after morning-light
to medo modig   siþþan morgenleoht   604

buoyant in mood,   a mead-cup bore
mode geþungen   medoful ætbær   624

in this mead-hall   mine abide
onþisse meoduhealle   minne gebidan   638

many a mead-bench   as I hear tell
medubenc monig   mine gefræge   776

mead-path measured   with a group of maids
medostigge mæt   mægþa hose   924

many a mead-cup   their kinsmen
medoful manig   magasþara   1015

on the mead-bench   treasure gave
onþære medubence   maþðum gesealde   1052

along mead-bench   should tell
æfter medobence   mænan scolde   1067

with mood in company   mead-plains trod
modig on gemonge   meodowongas træd   1643

on mead-bench   by the treasure worthier
on meodubence   maþme þy weorþra   1902

with hearty words;   among mead-vessels turned
meaglum wordum;   meoduscencum hwearf   1980

more mead-happiness;   at times the famous queen
medudream maran;   hwilum mæru cwen   2016

nor him on mead-bench   worth much
ne hyne on medobence   micles wyrðne   2185

I that time remember   when we mead drank
icðæt mæl geman   þær we meduþegun   2633

man with his kinsmen   in mead-lodge dwell
mon mid his magum   meduseld buan   3065

On *ale* line 769: I believe with Smithers (*English and Germanic Studies* 4:75) that *ealuscerwen* is to be paired with the "obviously synonymous *meduscenc*" in line 1980. Could the *rw* of *scerw-*, here and once elsewhere, be emended to *nc*, making an obscure word into a common one? Formula theory, desiring a standardized diction, would welcome the change. The meaning "share" for *scerw-*, given by Smithers, is satisfactory, though; cf. the Homeric expression "equal feast" (*Il.* 1.468 and eleven other instances).

On *mead* line 69: for the reading "a great mead-lodge . . . which people should hear of forever," see Robinson (*Tennessee Studies in Literature* 11:155), exemplary scholarship.

On *mead* lines 924 and 1643: take *mead* in the sense "meadow"; emend the text as needed; note that we are not asked to believe in a beer-plain, a wine-path.

We were looking for a principle. What we have found is that one drinks mead in the beer-hall (2633–2635) and ale in the wine-hall (769–771). Is there any rhyme or reason? Was the poet hoodwinking us (for our entertainment and his), or was he negligent? I believe his intentions will be best shown by comparative theory (involving Homer), and by set theory (explaining *beer, ale, wine,* and *mead* as a group, rather than individually).

Words may be wholly synonymous, like *furze, gorse,* and *whin.* Or they may be merely similar in meaning, rough synonyms. Or they may have little to do with each other, or nothing. No guidelines are evident beforehand. To make a beginning, mark the forms *woinos* and *methu,* sisters of our *wine* and *mead:*

we sat feasting on meat in abundance and sweet liquor (*methu*),
for not yet was the crimson wine (*woinos*) used up from our ships
(*Od.* 9.162–163)

the son of Jason had given liquor *(methu)* to be fetched, a thousand measures;
from there the long-haired Achaeans brought wine *(woinizonto)* *(Il.* 7.471–742)

Clearly, there is no distinction between *woinos* and *methu* here; they are synonymous, or the next thing to it. There may be a distinction between them elsewhere, though. And either word may have come to mean such and such in this locale, but such and such else in that one, as *dbs* is grape juice (mother of wine) in Arabic, but honey (mother of mead) in Hebrew. So from the Homeric terms and the Semitic analogue, we conclude—what? That *wine* and *mead* tend now to converge, now to diverge; they are the same or they are different, depending on who you are and where and when.

Truly, a spectrum of sense may be broad. Consider our word *fu☆k*, whose nakedness I have fig-leaved. *A Supplement to the Oxford English Dictionary* (1972) says "ulterior etym. unknown," just as Chantraine says "pas d'étymologie assurée" for the Greek word *pugē* "rump, backside." Solve both problems at once: the two forms are cognate by Grimm's law, English *f* answering to Greek *p* as in *feet, podes,* and English *k* to Greek *g* as in *kin, genos.* Is the brimstone of sodomy in our nostrils? No, it is a matter of posture in heterosexual union, at least mainly. When a word can vary as widely as this one has done (for it is a single word only, in different guises, as *death* and *thanatos* are a single word, or *hemp* and *cannabis*), then *wine* may have been more variable in Old English than we should have guessed, and so may *mead* have been.

Wine and *mead* meant about the same, and the sense of each was unstable, general rather than specific. *Beer* and *ale,* in like fashion, meant the same; other languages use the one or the other; German has only *beer,* Norwegian only *ale.* If then *wine* is roughly synonymous with *mead,* and *beer* synonymous with *ale,* how much do these two have in common with those two? Today, beer and ale, brewed with hops, are bitter. Before the sixteenth century, in England, they were unhopped and sweetish (*Oxford English Dictionary* "hop"). So the difference between the one pair and the other is wider now than it used to be. I will not say that beer and ale, wine and mead, came from the same barrel, in the days of Canute and Chogilaicus; but I am inclined to think so.

I say only that beer and ale, wine and mead, came from the same barrel in *Beowulf*. Why did the poet confound them, rather than create distinctions among them? In Old English prosody, as the passages quoted illustrate, the two halves of a line were joined by alliteration (about which nothing need be said, except that any vowel would alliterate with any other, *a*pples and *o*ranges). A poet expressed his thought now with this sound, now with that one. Sometimes he would say *lake*, sometimes *mere* or *holm* or *sea*; to him they meant nearly enough the same that the choice among them could be determined by sound, rather than by sense. Sometimes he would say *ship*, at other times *boat* or *wood* or *keel*, or *floater* or *naca*. How do you speak of a thimble, alliterating on *f*? Our German cousins say *finger-hat*. How do you speak of a mushroom, alliterating on *t*? When a solution was discovered, it would be used again, and lose its morning freshness: a shame that we no longer visualize the *toad-stool*. Every concept was to be denoted now with this alliteration, now with that. Sense was one parameter, sound another; where they intersected lay the term suiting the context. How do you tell of beer or ale, alliterating on *w* or *m*, if not with *wine* or *mead*? Once a poet had amassed his thesaurus—with *beer*, *ale*, *wine*, and *mead* as one group of synonyms, and with a hundred similar groups—he could create mightier songs than before. And the same is true for Homer, mutatis mutandis. Why did the poet, composing in dactylic hexameters, usually say *woinos* but sometimes *methu*, in speaking of wine (or mead)? Because *woinos* usually, but *methu* sometimes, had the rhythm he desired; not for any other reason.

There had to be a ready answer to every problem, but not a number of answers. Homer spoke of the "much-thundering sea" *poluphloisboio thalassēs* eight times, and of the "sea broad-for-sailing-on" *thalassēs euruporoio* three times; the phrases have the same case and length and position in the line, and each begins with a single consonant; nor does the epithet in either occur elsewhere in the *Iliad* or the *Odyssey*. It is interesting that neither has managed to oust the other. Similarly in *Beowulf* three phrases—"over swan-road" *ofer swanrade* (200), "over sea-billows" *ofer sæwylmas* (393), and "over salt-water" *ofer sealt wæter* (1989)—fill entire half lines alliterating once on *s*. It would seem that any one of them might have replaced the other two.

There is a like instance in the Homeric expressions for wine. The accusative phrases (long *kai*) *woinon eruthron* (*Od*. 12.327) and *(te) woinon eruthron* (*Od*. 16.444) have been replaced by (long *kai*) *aithopa woinon* in *Il*. 24.641 and *(te) aithopa woinon* in *Od*. 2.57. In theory there is no duplication: *aithopa woinon* "blazefaced wine," beginning with a vowel, ought to shorten a preceding vowel; *woinon eruthron* "crimson wine," beginning with a consonant, ought not. But the preceding vowel here—*Il*. 24.641, *Od*. 2.57—was not to be shortened; *woinon eruthron* would have served as well in these lines as *aithopa woinon*, indeed better. The economy has been violated, the gears have not meshed, minor though the flaw may be. What then of wine in *Beowulf*? There is no trace of redundancy; *wine, mead, beer*, and *ale* have silenced their rivals.

How well did the Anglo-Saxons know *either* wine or mead, once they had left continental Europe for an island unfriendly to the grape, and once the flower-bearing bee-nurturing meadows had been cleared for the growing of grain? It is a question not to be answered from the poetry. The *words* were familiar, whatever they might denote, for poets kept them alive. If wine and mead had been left behind on the migration to England, they still had to be spoken of, for there was still a need to express *beer* or *ale* alliterating on *w* or *m*. Customs could change, but the poetic tradition would not—not until its wants were supplied in a new fashion. This is a conclusion of basic worth, and it can be reached by another path.

The Anglo-Saxons once believed in *god, lord, father, wyrd*, and *metod*—terms perhaps not wholly synonymous, but capable of being often used one for another. They also believed in the powers we remember with our weekdays. Then Christianity made its conquest, not with Carolingian beheadings but with re-interpretation. The conversion was to be a reformation, not a revolution. Tiw, Woden, and Thunor had to be removed, condemned as devils. *God, lord*, and *father* were kept, but given, little by little, a Levantine sense to replace the Nordic one. Christ would come soon, when the way had been prepared. So much may be surmised from *Beowulf*, in comparison on the one hand with Old Norse poetry, and on the other with Old English poetry of a more intense Christian colour. Now *wyrd* and *metod*, truly Germanic and heathen, not at all Hebraic or Hellenistic, why were not they too driven underground, along with Tiw and that lot? Because poets, even if au courant in religious thought, were old-fashioned in their craft. Ancient resources for referring to the almighty could not be given up until equally valuable new resources were available. *Wyrd* and *metod* were locked in the language by the need to alliterate on *w* and *m*, just as *wine* and *mead* were.

Synonyms made alliterating easier, and also made the poetry more challenging, more interesting. I would hate to say whether there was, or was not, a difference between a chemise and a blouse. Similarly with the audience as they heard of ale drunk from wine-flagons, and of mead-fights in the beer-hall. Meanwhile, the Homeric audience was hearing of *woinos* called *methu*. Still, the two traditions differ. In Homer (for the sake of the rhythm) a common or proper noun, though sometimes replaced, was more characteristically modified. Wine might become mead, but it might become blazefaced wine or crimson wine. In Old English (for the sake of alliteration) the common or proper noun was almost always replaced, seldom modified. Rather than being described, the wine was transmuted. The result is, the *Iliad* has a non-Beowulfian clarity, and *Beowulf* has a non-Iliadic murkiness. What is a "sea broad-for-sailing-on," from Homer? It is a sea; the question was not worth asking. What is a swan-road, from our own epic? It is a sea too; the question was more of a riddle. Who are "king of men Agamemnon" and "Gerenian horseman Nestor"? They are Agamemnon and Nestor. Who are the "giver of treasure" and the "man blest in victory"? Who indeed?

Phrases for the Homeric heroes are highly specific; not only is "king of men Agamemnon" (used forty-four times in the *Iliad*) limited to Agamemnon perforce, but even the descriptive element "king of men" is used for scarcely anyone else (and for no-one else more than once). The phrases are also unchanging; they take no account of time; Agamemnon and Nestor are described in the

Odyssey (where in fact Agamemnon is a ghost) just as they were in the *Iliad*, and the same is true of Achilles, and of Menelaus and Helen. Phrases for the heroes of *Beowulf*, though, are not specific but generic, and are not unchanging but variable with age or rank. In the earlier part of the poem, in half-line phrases alliterating on *h* . . . *h* or *f*, Hrothgar is a "hoary battle-warrior" *har hilderinc* and "shepherd of the people" *folces hyrde*, while Beowulf is the "hero battle-fierce" *hæle hildedeor* and "foot-champion" *feþecempa;* in the latter part, with a shift on *h* . . . *h* and *f*, Beowulf is a *har hilderinc* and *folces hyrde*, Wiglaf being the *hæle hildedeor* and *feþecempa*. We may imagine an episode earlier yet, with Hrothgar as a "hero battle-fierce" and "foot-champion," and an episode later yet, with Wiglaf as the "hoary battle-warrior" and "shepherd of the people."

A problem is whether "the pathos of aging and the mystery of the hero's inevitable departure from this life acquire deeper poignancy through these verbal echoes that emphasize the rhythmic recurrence of such events in the heroic past" (Robinson in *Old English Poetry* pp. 144–145). For two reasons I doubt whether we hear the "verbal echoes" as the poem is recited, or even when it is read aloud. First, elements like *har hilderinc* "hoary battle-warrior"—though restricted by the alliteration—occur fairly often. Hrothgar and Beowulf are not the only hoary battle-warriors; Byrhtnoth in the "Battle of Maldon" is another, and Constantine in the "Battle of Brunanburh" yet another. The title "shepherd of the people" is used in the epic for Hrothgar and Beowulf and others as well, and in the "Battle of Finnsburh" and the "Meters of Boethius" besides. Who have the title "hero battle-fierce"? Not Beowulf and Wiglaf alone, but Andrew in "Andreas" and Judas in "Elene," too. If a phrase occurred just two or three times, and in *Beowulf* only, we might—at least as compilers, if not as ordinary listeners or readers—collocate those instances. But when we take account of the "Battle of Maldon" and the "Battle of Finnsburh" and "Andreas," we usually find that a phrase was a familiar one in its day. Think also of the poetry that has perished without trace, as *Beowulf* almost did. If all those poems had survived, there would have been dozens and dozens of hoary battle-warriors, a compendious Almanach de Gotha. No-one but a scholar would associate

Beowulf with Hrothgar, as one *har hilderinc* with another, even nowadays, and no-one at all would have done so in the age of the scop.

My second reason for denying that we hear verbal echoes is that most of us grasp the idea without remembering the particular words. If Hrothgar is a "hoary battle-warrior" *har hilderinc*, an "old home-warden" *eald ðelweard*, or a "giver of treasure" *sinces brytta*, and if Beowulf becomes something similar later on, we may be aware of the resemblance between them; but we do not really recall, without being prompted, *which* term was used earlier. Was it "hoary battle-warrior," or "old home-warden," or "giver of treasure," or was it perhaps "lord of earls" *eorla dryhten*, or "gold-friend of men" *goldwine gumena*? Each of these left very nearly the same impression as the others. What are the phrases that describe Beowulf at first and Wiglaf afterwards? One is "foot-champion" *feþecempa*, and another is "hero battle-fierce" *hæle hildedeor*. How about "ruthless champion" *reþe cempa*, "noble of ancient lineage" *æþeling ærgod*, "man blest in victory" *sigoreadig secg*, and "man keen in deeds" *dædcene mon*? Not every Old Anglist will be able to say which two or three of these are used for both of the young warriors. If our memory tells us that the poet said such and such when he actually said something equivalent, then we are just humming the right tune in the wrong key, which is what we usually do, as Barlow and Morgenstern (*A Dictionary of Musical Themes*) were aware. The terms "noble of ancient lineage" and "man blest in victory" meant roughly the same (a warrior not a king); "whale-road" and "swan-road" meant the same; *ale* and *mead* meant the same; and so did "good war-king" *god guðcyning* and "giver of rings" *beaga brytta*. Is it agreed? For those who would deny the synonymy I will mention one or two of the greatest mistakes ever made in literature.

The poetry of the Old Testament depends upon the parallelism in meaning of consecutive hemistichs. It is a primary requirement, analogous to the alliteration of Old English, or to the dactylic hexameter of Homer. The stichs are apt to be synonymous, and they are generally connected by the particle *waw*, translated variously as *and, but, for, as*, or whatever else may be needed. A not uncommonly good specimen is: "he hath borne our griefs, and carried our sorrows." The Semitic flavour here is strong, as the Germanic flavour of "foamy-necked floater" is strong, or the Homeric flavour of "sea broad-for-sailing-on." Such expressions are recognized by the theorist as fulfilments of prosodic requirements. But our chief impression as we read or listen is one of amazement and pleasure at the opulence. It would for simple communication have sufficed to say "he hath borne our griefs" and "ship" and "sea." What we ought to do with the luxury is bask and bathe in it. If we are suspicious, we may distinguish between elements that mean the same, to our undoing.

My chief illustration is from the book of Judges. Because so many stichs and word pairs recur in Old Testament poetry, and also because some pairs were not only Hebraic but Ugaritic as well (see Dahood trans. *Psalms* vol. 3 pp. 445–456), we may regard every stich or pair as being, more probably than not, older than any poem it now appears in. And similarly we may regard every poem as being older than its own context. Our judgment would then be that the Song of Deborah preceded its framework. We should say this even if none of the stichs or pairs from the Song recurred elsewhere, but we are the more confident seeing that some of the stichs and pairs do recur. A segment at the beginning of the Song (Judg. 5.4–5) recurs in the Psalms (68.7–8); and the pairs "milk" ḥālāb/ "butter" ḥem'āh (Judg. 5.25, Deut. 32.14) and "hand" yād/" right hand" yāmîn (Judg. 5.26, Ps. 89.13, 89.25, 130.10, Isa. 48.13) recur as well. Assume then that the most famous incident had poetic form before it was put into prose:

> Blessed above women shall Jael the wife of Heber the Kenite be, blessed shall she be above women in the tent. He asked water, and she gave him milk, she brought forth butter in a lordly dish. She put her hand to the nail, and her right hand to the workmen's hammer; and with the hammer she smote Sisera, she smote off his head, when she had pierced and stricken through his temples. At her feet he bowed, he fell he lay down: at her feet he bowed, he fell: where he bowed, there he fell down dead. (Judg. 5.24–27)

And Jael went out to meet Sisera, and said unto him, Turn in, my lord, turn in to me; fear not. And when he had turned in unto her into the tent, she covered him with a mantle. And he said unto her, Give me, I pray thee, a little water to drink; for I am thirsty. And she opened a bottle of milk, and gave him drink, and covered him. Again he said unto her, Stand in that door of the tent, and it shall be, when any man doth come and enquire of thee, and say, Is there any man here? that thou shalt say, No. Then Jael Heber's wife took a nail of the tent, and took an hammer in her hand, and went softly unto him, and smote the nail into his temples, and fastened it into the ground: for he was fast asleep and weary. So he died. (Judg. 4.18–21)

The great difference between the two accounts is that Sisera was killed standing in the one, but lying down in the other. How can we start to explain it? The words translated as *nail* and *hammer* are obscure, their sense uncertain; so render them with *mauler* and *clout*. Avoid the unjustified iteration of *hand*, and find for the *waw* a particle more nearly meaningless. The poetry now reads: "She put her grasp to the mauler, even her hand to the clout." Each word pair consists of two synonyms: *a single action has been told of twice.* The prosateur misunderstood his model! He thought a weapon was held by the one hand, a tool by the other. So the simple action told of twice became a complex action told of once! And Sisera who had been killed standing became killed as he was lying down.

Are we not presumptuous? do we modern Occidentals fathom synonymous parallelism better than an author from the culture that produced it did? Wellhausen, whom I have followed, clinched his brilliant discussion *(Die Composition des Hexateuchs und der historischen Bücher* 3rd ed. pp. 217–218) with a like instance of misunderstanding from the gospels. First, the prophecy: "behold, thy King cometh unto thee: he is just, and having salvation; lowly, and riding upon an ass, and upon a colt the foal of an ass" (Zech. 9.9). Surely, one animal, not two. Now, the fulfilment: "And the disciples went, and did as Jesus commanded them, And brought the ass, and the colt, and put on them their clothes, and they set him thereon" (Mt 21.7). Two animals here, not one. Were we to picture Jesus as sitting upon both of them?

Among the teachings of the bible, to the philologist, are these exempla against failing to see synonyms for what they are. Anyone who distinguishes between an "old home-warden" *eald ǽelweard* and a "hoary battle-warrior" *har hilderinc*, or between *ale* and *mead*, hearing much where little was intended, will be at fault, though in the best of company. We who do not make such distinctions fail to remember whether the one term was used, or the other. Verbal echoes, which are always faint except when they are expected (as in a refrain), are especially faint—in fact, inaudible—when one synonym interferes with another. What we do perhaps sense is the shadow of a recollection of an idea; there may be a glimmering of a thought that earlier impressed us mightily. When so and so is said to bestow largesse, or to drink a flask of liquor, it will occasionally fleet across our mind that someone else did much the same before. But we do not remember just which word was used for the largesse, or just what kind of liquor it was.

I would not close without saying that general principles may at times be laid aside. When there is to be a connotation of wormwood and agony, as in *Beowulf* 769 and *Andreas* 1526, Stanley (in *Continuations and Beginnings* p. 111) takes *ale* to be the right word, *mead* the wrong one. I disagree, but do see something to utter in support of his cause. In all good poetry there is the likelihood of a tour de force, even with the use of the most traditional materials. Among the biblical word pairs (lying at hand since we have just been looking at them), there are several in which, though the two members mean much the same, one is greater than the other. An example is "mountain" har/"hill" gib'āh. Sometimes these are used as if synonymous: "I will get me to the mountain of myrrh, and to the hill of frankincense" (S./Sol. 4.6), where both hemistichs refer to the same part of a woman's body, which we generally speak of in Latin. But usually these terms exhibit staircase parallelism: "The mountains skipped like rams, and the little hills like lambs" (Ps. 114.4), where the large things go together, and the small things together. This is charming, not remarkable. And as with "mountain/hill" so with "gold" zāhāb/"silver" kesep. Sometimes they are synonymous, sometimes they differ in degree. But in combination with the equally formulaic word pairs "iron/brass" and "stone/wood," the matching is not by worth, but by *colour*: "For brass I will bring gold, and for iron I will bring silver, and for wood brass, and for stones iron" (Isa. 60.17). This is remarkable truly. What shall we say of the parallelism in the verse "Or ever the silver cord be loosed, or the golden bowl be broken" (Ecclesiastes 12.6)? The larger passage is about the failing of our members as old age comes upon us, "in the day when the keepers of the house shall tremble, and the strong men shall bow themselves, and the grinders cease because they are few, and those that look out of the windows be darkened, and the doors shall be shut in the streets." What of the silver cord and the golden bowl? Unless I am mistaken the distich has to do with a spermatic thread (semen is close to silver in hue) and the urinary bladder (urine is golden). Precious metals used for their colour in synonymous or staircase *genito-urinary* parallelism! A once-in-a-lifetime composition, powerful and gorgeous, but sounding familiar since "gold/silver" was a pair so well known.

I argue by analogy. If there are antitraditional tours in other formulaic poems, there may be some in *Beowulf*. Once in a lifetime *ale* and *mead* can have been used with an alertness to the difference in sense between them. Still, my opinion is that the poets never did distinguish between the meanings of those terms, nor between the meanings of *beer* and *wine*. Nor does it seem to me likely that an early audience would have been aware of any such distinction.

Was not then the choice among *beer, ale, wine,* and *mead* influenced in any way by the month of the year, or the hour of the day, or by one's age or sex?

If the seasons are blossomtime, midsummer, autumn, and wintertime, what beverages do you drink in them?

If you are an epic figure, what do you drink upon waking? what at mealtime? what in the afternoon? what at bedtime?

If men drink mead and women wine, what do the elderly drink? what do babies drink?

Strong Drink in Beowulf

Beer, ale, wine, and *mead* have affinities with the words for the times, persons, objects, and events that alliterate with them. In *b*lossomtime drink *b*eer, in *m*idsummer drink *m*ead, upon *w*aking drink *w*ine, and so forth. The examples were made up, but they are of a kind with ones from the poem. Though beer-drinkers are blithe (617), mead-drinkers get moody (604, 624, 1643), ale-drinkers get angry (769), and wine leads to weapons (1467). Not a mead-hall, but a wine-hall, is windy (2456) and lies under the welkin (714). If you are serving an earl, do not give him beer, give him ale (769).

The members of my family drink whiskey.

Answers

I. The last supper and the meals of remembrance or fellowship

A. Was the fellowship meal known as a "(feast of) charity"?

For a good while, the early Christians kept (loosely associated with the sacrament) a feast of charity, denoted by the word *agapē*, seemingly as in Jude 12 (2 Peter 2.13 is similar, but has *apatē* "deception" instead). The original reading though is *achatē* "agate." The New Testament merely uses the proverb "mole in a gemstone," as we can show from the *Lithica* ascribed to Orpheus.

B. Was the last supper, was Jesus on the cross, a passover?

The synoptic gospels regard the last supper as a passover meal; the fourth gospel regards Jesus on the cross as a passover sacrifice. In symbol, he is now the passover bread, now the passover lamb. The central event of the Old Testament is the type; the passion of Jesus, the antitype. Both of the gospel accounts depend on the etymologizing of *pascha* (an unintelligible Aramaic word in the Septuagint) as *paschein* "suffer."

C. Was the last supper meant to be renewed in remembrance?

The gospels do not say that Jesus bade his followers to renew the last supper. The authority that Christians follow in doing so is 1 Corinthians 11. Why was the remembrance more important to Paul than to the evangelists? Because to him especially, the types and antitypes composed a grand design. Now that all the promises had been kept, why was the end delayed? If there were a sacrament, the aftertime could be accommodated—through a new typology—in the scheme of things. So the death of Jesus became not the final event, but the central one.

D. Is the Lord's supper compatible with modern science?

The main impediment to belief in God is the antediluvian world view of most religions. Better to define God from physics as the Law behind the working of things. Is there then no commerce between God and man? I would take Jesus as having had, by nature, greater force—and a deeper awareness—than anyone else has had. Through a meal of remembrance or fellowship I would be as his early followers were.

II. Does the *Inferno* have one higher sense, or three, or none?

In addition to its literal sense—its gallery of portraits from the afterlife—the *Commedia* may be held to have a pervasive moral sense in its diagrammatic arrangements of sins and virtues. It may also be held to have a pervasive anagogical sense in its wholesale allusion back to the life on earth; but the anagogical is continuous with, not distinct from, the literal sense, for last thoughts from this world have gone with the soul into the next. The 34th canto of the *Inferno* has also an allegorical (typological) sense: the group Lucifer, Judas, Brutus and Cassius, implies a grouping of God, Christ, and Caesar, who are each the supreme being. So there is but a single higher sense—the moral—if the anagogical, as being continuous with the literal, is not counted, and if the allegorical (typological), as being found in the 34th canto only, is not counted either; but to count all three would be fair. Our attention should though be given elsewhere. That the archfelons are damnable beyond all others both as judged by the ethical nature of their sin, and as judged from those they sinned against—this combining of primary reasons is the best piece of workmanship in literature.

III. When in *Othello* is the marriage, when is the consummation?

The vows were exchanged (evidently) just before the play begins; but the wedding night, in Act 1, is interrupted, and so is the postponed wedding night, in Act 2. The marriage is never consummated; the wedding sheets, which by the Moorish custom would have been the tokens of Desdemona's virginity, are never stained with her blood: these matters we were meant to be aware of, but not to think about; for they are spoken of, but not directly.

IV. When in *Beowulf* is beer drunk, or mead, when ale or wine?

It is striking that thanes may drink ale from a wine-flask in the beer-hall. To compose alliterative verse easily, the poet had a set of synonyms for every major concept. *Mead, beer, wine,* and *ale* were such a set. The audience might have found, and we as readers are apt to find, distinctions among these words; but the maker of the poetry did not intend them. If *mead*, but not wine, is drunk in the *morning*, that is because of the alliteration.

Bibliographical index

Allen, Ned B., "The Two Parts of *Othello*," *Shakespeare Survey* 21 (1968) 13–29: 76

Andreas Capellanus, *The Art of Courtly Love*, ed. Frederick W. Locke (New York 1957): 57

Auerbach, Erich, "Figurative Texts Illustrating Certain Passages of Dante's *Commedia*," *Speculum* 21 (1946) 474–489: 64

——, *Mimesis*, trans. Willard R. Trask (Princeton 1953): 51, 56, 64

——, *Scenes from the Drama of European Literature* (New York 1959), incl. the essay "Figura," trans. Ralph Manheim: 51

Barlow, Harold, and Sam Morgenstern, *A Dictionary of Musical Themes* (New York 1948): 92

Barr, James, *Fundamentalism* (Philadelphia 1977): 13

Beare, Francis Wright, *The Gospel According to Matthew* (Oxford 1981): 20

Bergin, Thomas G., *Dante* (Boston 1965): 49, 57

Bertram, Georg, *Die Leidengeschichte Jesu und der Christuskult* (Göttingen 1922): 17

Bigg, Charles, ed. *Epistles of St. Peter and St. Jude* (Edinburgh 1901), the International Critical Commentary: 12

Black, Matthew, *An Aramaic Approach to the Gospels and Acts* 2nd ed. (Oxford 1954): 18

Boose, Lynda E., "Othello's Handkerchief," *English Literary Renaissance* 5 (1975) 360–374: 68

Brandeis, Irma, *The Ladder of Vision* (London 1960): 55

Brugnoli, Giorgio, Introductory essay on the letter to Cangrande, in vol. 2, pp. 512–521, of Dante's *Opere minori* (Milan 1979): 45

Bundy, Walter E., *Jesus and the First Three Gospels* (Cambridge, Mass. 1955): 27

Burckhardt, John Lewis, *Arabic Proverbs* 2nd ed. (London 1875): 69

Callahan, J. J., "The Curvature of Space in a Finite Universe," *Scientific American* vol. 235, Aug. 1976, pp. 90–100: 41

Carlyle, John Aitken, trans. *The Inferno of Dante* (London 1900), the Temple Classics: 53 and elsewhere

Chantraine, Pierre, *Dictionnaire étymologique de la langue grecque* vol. 3 (Paris 1968): 87

Cross, Frank Moore, Jr., *The Ancient Library of Qumran and Modern Biblical Studies* (New York 1958): 25

Cupitt, Don, *The Debate about Christ* (London 1979): 34

Dahood, Mitchell, trans. *Psalms* (New York 1970), the Anchor Bible: 93

Dalman, Gustaf, *Jesus—Jeshua*, trans. Paul P. Levertoff (London 1929), S.P.C.K.: 19

Daniel, P. A., "A Time-Analysis of the Plots of Shakspere's Plays," *The New Shakspere Society's Transactions* 1877–9, pp. 117–346: 76

De Sanctis on Dante, ed. Joseph Rossi and Alfred Galpin (Madison 1957): 61–62

Dean, Leonard F., *A Casebook on "Othello"* (New York 1961): 76

Denniston, J. D., and Denys Page, ed. Aeschylus, *Agamemnon* (Oxford 1957): 71

Driver, S. R., ed. *Exodus* (Cambridge 1911), Cambridge Bible for Schools and Colleges: 22

Galton, Dorothy, letter in *Times Literary Supplement* 19 March 1971, p. 325: 82

Gamow, George, "The Evolutionary Universe," *Scientific American* vol. 195, Sept. 1956, pp. 136–154: 37

Ginzburg, V. L., *Key Problems of Physics and Astrophysics*, trans. Oleg Glebov (Moscow 1976): Preface

Grandgent, C. H., ed. *La Divina commedia di Dante Alighieri* (Boston 1933): 60

Granville-Barker, Harley, *Prefaces to Shakespeare* vol. 4, paperback ed. (Princeton 1965): 76

Grayson, Cecil, "Dante's Theory and Practice of Poetry," in *The World of Dante*, ed. Cecil Grayson (Oxford 1980): 64

Green, H. Benedict, *The Gospel according to Matthew* (Oxford 1975), New Clarendon Bible: 32

Herford, C. H., ed. *Othello* (Boston 1924), Arden ed. rev.: 76

Hinds, Edward A., "Parity and Time-Reversal Invariance in Atoms," *American Scientist* 69 (1981) 430–436: 39

Holden, Constance, "Identical Twins Reared Apart," *Science* vol. 207, 21 March 1980, pp. 1323–1328: 40

Jaubert, Annie, "La date de la dernière Cène," *Revue de l'histoire des religions* 146 (1954) 140–173: 17

Jeremias, Joachim, *The Eucharistic Words of Jesus*, trans. Arnold Ehrhardt (Oxford 1955): 16–17

Inconsistencies

Tasker, R. V. G., ed. *The Greek New Testament* being the text trans. in the New English Bible (Oxford and Cambridge 1964): 11, 32

Thomas, Lewis, *The Medusa and the Snail* (New York 1979), pp. 76–81 "On Warts": 40

Toynbee, Paget, ed. *Dantis Alagherii epistolae* (Oxford 1920): 44

——, *A Dictionary of Proper Names and Notable Matters in the Works of Dante* (Oxford 1898): 55

Wellhausen, J., *Die Composition des Hexateuchs und der historischen Bücher des alten Testaments* 3rd ed. (Berlin 1899): 94

Westcott, Brooke Foss, and Fenton John Anthony Hort, ed. *The New Testament in the Original Greek* (New York 1957): 32

Wilczek, Frank, "The Cosmic Asymmetry between Matter and Antimatter," *Scientific American* vol. 243, Dec. 1980, pp. 82–90: 39

Index of subjects

affinities in Old English between words of like alliteration: 97

agape: see *feast of charity*

ale: unhopped, 87; see *strong drink*

allegorical (typological) etymologizing of *pascha*: 18–21; before or after the gospels were written, 19

allegory: its broad meaning, 42–45; see *anagogical sense, fourfold sense, moral sense, typology,* and *typology of Judas*

anagogical sense: 42–45, 48–50, 53–64, 67; see *literal-anagogical continuum*

beer: unhopped, 87; see *strong drink*

blood: shed at the loss of virginity, 68; the words "yet I'll not shed her blood" intelligible only if the marriage has not been consummated, 75; see *tokens of virginity*

breadth of meaning, words varying with local preference: *dbs*, 87; *fu☆k*, 87

chastity of Desdemona: 68, 70, 74, 79

contraction: see *expansion*

Deuteronomy 22, of threefold interest for *Othello*: 68, 81

dbs: see *breadth of meaning*

epithet, Homeric: see *illustration of the epithet*

errors corrigible by altering a letter or two: spots on a (feast of) charity, 12; potter in the temple, 27

etymologizing of psḥ: 17, 18; see *allegorical (typological) etymologizing of "pascha"*

existence of God: by definition rather than from proof, 37–39

expansion of one into two, or contraction of two into one: to make rough wording smooth, 12; to simplify Hebrew poetry, 45; by a misunderstanding of Hebrew poetry, 94

(feast of) charity: and the sacrament, 9–10;

female impersonation: see *Deuteronomy 22*

fourfold sense: found variously by Augustine and Aquinas, 42; defined variously in the *Convivio* and the letter to Cangrande, 43; in the 34th canto, 64–67

fu☆k: see *breadth of meaning*

half-awareness, our: that the marriage has not been consummated, 78–79;

sheets: see *tokens of virginity*
sinfulness: sometimes shown in hell, sometimes not, 55–61
strong drink: and alliteration in Old English, 89–90; and meter in Homer, 88
synonyms: in Old English, 88; our inability to remember which one was used before, 92; misunderstanding of, in scripture, 94; see *strong drink* and *heroes, phrases for in Old English*
tokens of virginity, the Moorish custom, spoken of in Deuteronomy 22: 68–69, 75, 77, 79; see *handkerchief*
tours de force: always possible in great poetry, 95–96
typology: threefold, of the last supper, 25–36; the fulfilling of forehappening, not of foretelling, 26; Paul's innovation, 31–36; Aquinas on, 43; originated (evidently) with Jesus himself, 46; Dante's innovation, 49; see *allegorical (typological) etymologizing of "pascha"* and *typology of Judas*
typology of Judas: the unworthy at the sacrament, 35–36; and Lucifer, Brutus and Cassius, in the *Inferno*, 65–66
violation of economy: in Homer, 88–89; in Old English, 88–89
wedding night in *Othello*, interrupted twice: 70, 72, 76–77, 80
wine: see *strong drink*
wyrd and metod, comparable to wine and mead: 90